Bearing Witness

Bearing Witness

*Stories of Martyrdom and
Costly Discipleship*

Edited by Charles E. Moore and Timothy Keiderling
Introduction by John D. Roth and Elizabeth Miller

Plough Publishing House

Published by Plough Publishing House
Walden, New York
Robertsbridge, England
Elsmore, Australia
www.plough.com

Cover image: plainpicture/Demurez Cover Arts
All maps are from Wikimedia Commons (public domain)
ISBN: 978-087486-704-6
21 20 19 18 17 16   1 2 3 4 5 6

A catalog record for this book is available from the British Library.
Library of Congress Cataloging-in-Publication Data

Names: Moore, Charles E., 1956- editor.
Title: Bearing witness : stories of martyrdom and costly discipleship /
    edited by Charles E. Moore and Timothy Keiderling ; introduction by John
    D. Roth.
Description: Walden : Plough Pub. House, 2016.
Identifiers: LCCN 2015048622 (print) | LCCN 2015049546 (ebook) | ISBN
    9780874867046 (pbk.) | ISBN 9780874867053 (epub) | ISBN 9780874867060
    (mobi) | ISBN 9780874867077 (pdf)
Subjects: LCSH: Christian martyrs--Biography.
Classification: LCC BR1608.5 .B43 2016 (print) | LCC BR1608.5 (ebook) | DDC
    272.092/2--dc23
LC record available at http://lccn.loc.gov/2015048622

Printed in the United States of America

If any want to become my followers,
let them deny themselves and take up their cross and follow me.
For those who want to save their life will lose it,
and those who lose their life for my sake will find it.

Jesus of Nazareth

Contents

Introduction

John D. Roth and Elizabeth Miller

FOLLOWING JESUS CAN BE DANGEROUS. On April 14, 2014, members of Boko Haram, a radicalized Islamic group in Nigeria, attacked a girls' school in Chibok and kidnapped most of the students. Of the nearly three hundred young girls abducted, at least 178 were members of Ekklesiyar Yan'uwa a Nigeria (EYN), a Church of the Brethren group whose commitment to adult baptism and biblical nonresistance anchors them within the Anabaptist tradition. Since 2013, some ten thousand EYN members have been killed and many more have been forced to flee their homes.

For two millennia, Christians in every tradition have honored the memory of individuals and communities who have suffered, and often died, for reasons of faith. Anabaptist groups, for example, have long been inspired by *Martyrs Mirror*, a collection of stories and documents that begins with the crucifixion of Christ and concludes with detailed accounts of some fifteen hundred Anabaptists who were imprisoned, tortured, and killed for their faith during the sixteenth century.

The stories of costly discipleship recounted in this new collection – spanning the centuries from the early Christian church to the Radical Reformation to the contemporary global church – offer a fresh reminder that the decision to follow Christ can sometimes come at a price. Those of us involved with the Bearing Witness

John D. Roth is professor of history at Goshen College and director of the Institute for the Study of Global Anabaptism, which has given leadership to the Bearing Witness Stories Project. Elizabeth Miller serves as the administrative assistant of the Institute and manages the Bearing Witness website (martyrstories.org).

Stories Project think that these stories need to be told, and retold, for each generation, especially in light of the fact that for many in the global church today persecution is still a lived reality.

Since the stoning of Stephen, recorded in Acts 2, the Christian church has always honored those who have suffered or died in the name of Christ. Church fathers like Cyprian and Eusebius recognized the importance of gathering the stories of the apostles and other early Christians who suffered or died as *martyres* (witnesses) to their faith, trusting that these testimonies of faithfulness to Christ would inspire later generations. The template for early Christian martyrdom, of course, was Jesus. Though unjustly accused, he did not resort to violence to defend his cause, but bore his suffering with steadfastness and dignity. Yielding himself fully to God, Jesus forgave his accusers and accepted the humiliation of crucifixion in the knowledge that ultimately the resurrection would triumph over death.

On the surface, the qualifications for Christian martyrdom seem straightforward. Yet as the early church struggled to define orthodox belief, definitions of martyrdom became increasingly problematic. What, exactly, did a persecuted person need to believe in order to be accounted a Christian martyr? And who had the authority to make such a judgment? In the early fifth century, when the Donatists proclaimed as martyrs those members who were killed by Constantine for their alleged heresy, Augustine pushed back. It was "not the punishment," he declared, "but the cause that makes the martyr."

Augustine's statement became a standard point of reference for the Catholic Church in later centuries in its denial that dissenters such as John Wycliffe, Peter Waldo, or Jan Hus, who were all executed on charges of heresy, could rightfully be considered martyrs. The problem of definition became even more acute in the sixteenth century as the various religious traditions emerging out of the Reformation began to develop competing lists of martyrs, often commemorating as heroes individuals whom another tradition had pronounced heretical or seditious.

An additional challenge is the difficulty of separating the factual details surrounding an event from the simpler heroic narratives that emerged later. At their best, martyr stories help communities validate their own cultural identity. At their worst, these memories can serve to justify the resentment of one group against another and even lead to retribution.

In the Anabaptist tradition the martyrs have played a central role in the formation and sustaining of a collective identity – especially for groups such as the Amish, Mennonites, and Hutterites that immigrated to the United States and Canada in part to escape religious opposition in Europe and Russia. First emerging as a series of underground pamphlets, the Dutch accounts of Anabaptist martyrs eventually coalesced in the collection *Het Offer des Herren* (Sacrifice unto the Lord). Between 1562 and 1599, at least eleven editions appeared, often adding new martyr narratives, prison letters, or hymns.

With the publication of *Martyrs Mirror* in 1660, this dynamic tradition of martyr books came to an end and the canon of Anabaptist martyrs was virtually closed. Thieleman van Braght, a Dutch Mennonite minister from Haarlem and the compiler and author of *Martyrs Mirror*, opted for an inclusive definition of orthodoxy that could find support among all Anabaptist groups – namely, a commitment to believer's baptism and to defenselessness (or nonresistance) in the manner of Christ. (In selecting stories, the editors of this book have used similar criteria.) Van Braght hoped that *Martyrs Mirror* could serve as a shared point of reference and a source of unity within a fractious church. Thus, he devoted nearly half of the massive volume to a detailed argument tracing a line of Christians from the time of Christ to the present who had held to the principles of believer's baptism and nonresistance.

Ironically, by 1660 Anabaptists in the Netherlands were living in relative religious freedom and were participating fully in the artistic, economic, and cultural renaissance of the "Dutch Golden Age." Thus, instead of urging readers to hold firm in the face of persecution, van Braght warned of the seductions of wealth, social respectability, and political authority. For him, the martyr stories served as cautionary tales against the threat of acculturation.

So why do we in North America still need to tell martyr stories today? First, in the context of the extensive religious freedoms that North American believers now enjoy, the witness of the martyrs provides a useful reminder that following Jesus can still exact a cost. Their stories caution us, as citizens of a powerful "Christian" empire, against the temptation to justify violence in the name of Christ. They witness to the possibility of nonviolence and love of enemy even in the most extreme circumstances. And they call us to a life of compassion and humility, while reminding us that non-resistant love is not likely to be rewarded here on earth.

Furthermore, we should continue to tell stories of courageous witness because persecution is not just an ancient story but a contemporary reality. In most of the world outside of North America – specifically in Asia, Africa, and Latin America – Christianity is growing rapidly despite the fact that Christians in many countries are facing the painful reality of persecution and suffering. In fact, many of the contemporary stories in this collection come from churches and communities in these regions of the world.

A report issued in 2012 by the Center for the Study of Global Christianity estimates that in the twentieth century alone, around forty-five million Christians "lost their lives prematurely, in a situation of witness, as a result of human hostility." In addition, the report estimates that at least one hundred thousand Christians have been martyred each year since 2000. Clearly, bearing witness to Christ in the face of adversity, persecution, and suffering is not only an ancient memory in the Christian tradition – it is also an ongoing reality. Since Christians are called to bear one another's burdens (Gal. 6:2), wherever a part of the body is suffering because of its witness to Christ, the rest of the body must take heed. North American Christians need to tell stories of persecution and martyrdom because remaining silent, or willfully forgetting, or averting our attention from the reality of suffering, is simply unchristian.

Martyr stories prompt us to reexamine our own faith. If Christians in the West have tended to domesticate the faith – turning it into something safe or regarding it as an extension of our consumer tastes and preferences – encountering these stories should unsettle us and remind us that something of ultimate significance is at stake in the claim to be a follower of Jesus. Like the martyrs, we need to face life – and death – with the confidence that life is ultimately stronger than death and that history is always moving in the direction of the kingdom of God.

Martyr stories unite the church. Contemporary Christians should tell stories of faithfulness amid adversity – and especially the stories of brothers and sisters from the Global South – because doing so strengthens our sense of a shared identity. Christian communities come to know who they are by telling stories of God's faithfulness in the past and by locating themselves in continuity with a long narrative arc that goes all the way back to the story of the early church, the revelation of God in Christ, God's covenant with the children of Israel, and the account of creation itself. Remembering the martyrs is a way of extending the community of faith backward in time, reminding each congregation that it is not alone in its journey, but is joined in fellowship with faithful Christians throughout the history of the church.

Yet we also recognize that telling stories of suffering and death calls for a great deal of sensitivity. It is very important *how* such stories are told. Telling stories of contemporary Christian martyrs, for example, could harden existing stereotypes and prejudices against Muslims. Moreover, martyr stories can inadvertently glorify suffering, promote simplistic victim-offender dichotomies, encourage religious arrogance, or blind Christians to the power they wield within society. There is the danger, some have warned, that by focusing on a martyr tradition we encourage those who have suffered physical abuse to bear that pain in silence, or that we perpetuate pathologies that can result from an identity rooted in stories of suffering, trauma, and victimhood. Then there is the temptation that by focusing on martyr stories we ignore the many occasions in our own history where we Christians have been the perpetrators of injustice – for example, the Christian settlers who displaced indigenous peoples in the Americas.

These concerns must be taken seriously. But the solution to these dangers is not to reject history, or to stop telling martyr stories, or to think that we can escape from the burden of memory. Instead, the challenge, as theologian Miroslav Volf has argued, is to "remember rightly." In its most basic form, "right remembering" implies a conscious effort to acknowledge the complexity of every story, to gather as many sources as possible, to make those sources available to others, and to resist the temptation to invest the protagonists in the stories with more saintliness (or the antagonists with more evil) than the information at hand can reasonably support. Even martyrs whose actions at the time of their death we regard as exemplary are, on closer examination, deeply flawed people.

Right remembering also includes a commitment to tell the stories with an *empathetic* spirit – that is, a conversational posture committed to rethinking our history and theological commitments from the perspective of the other. Such a commitment is not easy. It requires an active engagement of the will, the intellect, and the imagination. And ultimately, truly empathetic understanding comes as a gift of the Holy Spirit. An empathetic understanding of the context does not justify the violence of those in power, nor does it exonerate historical actors from the moral consequences of their decisions. But right remembering does suggest that the way we tell the stories of those who suffered for their faith must be consistent with the compassion and love of enemy that we claim to uphold, even if doing so complicates the narrative.

Finally, right remembering means that we tell the martyr stories as a confession of faith. Christians who suffer and die for their faith bear witness to the lordship of Christ. Through their lives, their verbal witness, their perseverance, and their courage, martyrs point us to Christ – not just to the suffering that Christ endured, but also to the resurrection and the fundamental truth that life is more powerful than death. When Christians remember rightly, they confess their own desire to live in ways that are consistent with these truths. Thinking of the martyr stories as confession means that we will resist using them to explain or defend or argue for anything else.

With the hope of fostering a spirit of confession and connection among Anabaptists globally, the Institute for the Study of Global Anabaptism launched the Bearing Witness Stories Project in 2012. A dynamic and growing collection of stories of costly discipleship, the Bearing Witness Stories Project serves as a collection point for well-known martyr narratives as well as stories that may be beloved in a particular church conference but little known in the global church. Like van Braght's collection, *Bearing Witness* highlights stories that illustrate Christlike nonviolence in the face of opposition. We hope that these stories can both honor and serve the global church, connecting believers in prayer and thanksgiving across vast cultural, linguistic, and geographic distance. Rightly remembered, these stories can challenge Christians everywhere to a deeper understanding of discipleship, to closer relationships with congregations experiencing persecution today, and to greater courage in their own public witness.

Keeping these stories alive, and continuing to tell new stories, is an affirmation that those who relinquished their lives did not do so in vain. By recalling their deaths and the testimony of their lives, we affirm that history is meaningful, that our Christian faith has a purpose beyond mere self-preservation, that truth cannot be killed, and that the resurrection will ultimately triumph over the cross.

PART I

Early Christians

Stephen

died ca. AD 34, in Jerusalem

AFTER JESUS ROSE FROM THE DEAD and ascended into heaven, his disciples were filled with the Holy Spirit and went out into the street boldly proclaiming the resurrection. People came running from all over to see what was happening. One of the disciples, Peter, told them, "You, with the help of wicked men, put Jesus to death by nailing him to the cross. But God raised him from the dead, freeing him from the agony of death, because it was impossible for death to keep its hold on him." His listeners were "cut to the heart" with remorse for having joined the mob that called for Jesus' crucifixion. That very day three thousand of them were baptized and joined the disciples. The church was born.

When Peter healed a crippled man in the name of Jesus, news spread fast. The common people were thrilled that Jesus' miraculous powers were still at work in the world. Soon the sick and tormented were flocking to the apostles just as they had to Jesus, and many found healing. The religious leaders were jealous. They had the apostles thrown in jail. That night an angel appeared and led them right out without the guards noticing anything. "Go, stand in the temple courts," the angel said, "and tell the people all about this new life." The Book of Acts describes what happened next:

> When the high priest and his associates arrived, they called together the Sanhedrin – the full assembly of the elders of Israel – and sent to the jail for the apostles. But on arriving at the jail, the officers did not find them there. So they went back and reported, "We found the jail securely locked, with the guards standing at the doors; but when we opened them, we found no one inside." On hearing this report, the captain of the temple guard and the chief priests were at a loss, wondering what this might lead to.
>
> Then someone came and said, "Look! The men you put in jail are standing in the temple courts teaching the people." At that, the captain went with his officers and brought the apostles. They did not use force, because they feared that the people would stone them.
>
> The apostles were brought in and made to appear before the Sanhedrin to be questioned by the high priest. "We gave you strict orders not to teach in this name," he said. "Yet you have filled Jerusalem with your teaching and are determined to make us guilty of this man's blood."
>
> Peter and the other apostles replied: "We must obey God rather than men! The God of our ancestors raised Jesus from the dead – whom you killed by hanging him on a cross. God exalted him to his own right hand as Prince and Savior that he might bring Israel to repentance and forgive their sins. We are witnesses of these things, and so is the Holy Spirit, whom God has given to those who obey him."

When they heard this, they were furious and wanted to put them to death. But a Pharisee named Gamaliel, a teacher of the law, who was honored by all the people, stood up in the Sanhedrin and ordered that the men be put outside for a little while. Then he addressed the Sanhedrin: "Men of Israel, consider carefully what you intend to do to these men. Some time ago Theudas appeared, claiming to be somebody, and about four hundred men rallied to him. He was killed, all his followers were dispersed, and it all came to nothing. After him, Judas the Galilean appeared in the days of the census and led a band of people in revolt. He too was killed, and all his followers were scattered. Therefore, in the present case I advise you: Leave these men alone! Let them go! For if their purpose or activity is of human origin, it will fail. But if it is from God, you will not be able to stop these men; you will only find yourselves fighting against God."

His speech persuaded them. They called the apostles in and had them flogged. Then they ordered them not to speak in the name of Jesus, and let them go.

The number of followers of Jesus continued to grow. They gathered daily, bringing their food, money, and belongings for the apostles to distribute to the poor and sick among them. The apostles soon found that this administrative task was taking up too much of their time. They called everyone together and said, "It would not be right for us to neglect the ministry of the word of God in order to wait on tables. Brothers and sisters, choose seven men from among you who are known to be full of the Spirit and wisdom. We will turn this responsibility over to them and will give our attention to prayer and the ministry of the word."

One of the seven men the group chose was Stephen, "a man full of faith and of the Holy Spirit." The Bible says that Stephen, "full of God's grace and power, performed great wonders and signs among the people." His popularity soon won him enemies, but those who tried to argue with him proved no match against the wisdom he received from the Holy Spirit. His critics turned to treachery:

> They secretly persuaded some men to say, "We have heard Stephen speak blasphemous words against Moses and against God." So they stirred up the people and the elders and the teachers of the law. They seized Stephen and brought him before the Sanhedrin. They produced false witnesses, who testified, "This fellow never stops speaking against this holy place and against the law. For we have heard him say that this Jesus of Nazareth will destroy this place and change the customs Moses handed down to us."

"Are these charges true?" the high priest demanded. Instead of giving a straightforward answer, Stephen responded by passionately recounting the whole story of God's plan to save his people, from Abraham, Isaac, and Jacob through Moses and David. We don't know if his listeners were captivated or if they were growing increasingly impatient. Stephen ended with these words:

> You stiff-necked people! Your hearts and ears are still uncircumcised. You are just like your ancestors: You always resist the Holy Spirit! Was there ever a prophet your ancestors did not persecute? They even killed those who predicted the coming of the Righteous One. And now you have betrayed and murdered him – you who have received the law that was given through angels but have not obeyed it.

The Book of Acts reports what happened next:

> When the members of the Sanhedrin heard this, they were furious and gnashed their teeth at him. But Stephen, full of the Holy Spirit, looked up to heaven and saw the glory of God, and Jesus standing at the right hand of God. "Look," he said, "I see heaven open and the Son of Man standing at the right hand of God."

At this they covered their ears and, yelling at the top of their voices, they all rushed at him, dragged him out of the city and began to stone him. . . .

While they were stoning him, Stephen prayed, "Lord Jesus, receive my spirit." Then he fell on his knees and cried out, "Lord, do not hold this sin against them." When he had said this, he fell asleep.

To this day, Stephen is remembered as the first disciple of Jesus to follow in his master's footsteps by laying down his life for the sake of truth. Many more martyrs would soon follow. But new seeds had been planted that day. Those who stoned Stephen asked Saul, a young man standing by, to hold their coats for them. Before long Saul would himself become a great witness to Jesus, carrying the good news to new lands and peoples.

2

Polycarp

*died ca. AD 155, in Smyrna
(Izmir in modern Turkey)*

WHEN A YOUNG CHRISTIAN named Irenaeus first encountered the elderly Polycarp teaching in the metropolis of Smyrna, he was captivated.

It's not hard to understand why. According to Irenaeus, Bishop Polycarp was one of the few living disciples of the apostle John, who was the "beloved disciple" of Jesus himself. Polycarp preached what he had learned directly from eyewitnesses of Jesus. His connection with Christ's first apostles served as a bridge between the first generation of believers and those who followed, including influential thinkers and theologians such as Irenaeus, who would live to be a prominent church father in his own right.

Polycarp led the church in Smyrna with wisdom and authority, having been appointed to leadership by men who had seen and heard the Lord. He was frequently called on to settle disputes or correct false teaching. Even the other leaders of the early church valued his insight. When Polycarp visited Rome, the bishop there deferred to him regarding when to celebrate the Lord's Supper, as a sign of honor and respect.

Heeding John's warnings against false teachers, Polycarp faithfully defended the apostles' teaching against early heretics, including one Marcion, who held that the God of the Old Testament and the Father of Jesus were separate entities. Polycarp could be fiery, particularly when faced with such dangerous errors. In their only face-to-face meeting, Marcion asked, "Do you know me?"

"I know you, you firstborn of Satan!" Polycarp replied.

He was able to turn many away from such heresies, and thus strengthen the church's witness.

But Polycarp's work as a pastor and leader would not continue freely. When persecution broke out in Smyrna, some Christians were rounded up for interrogation, and required to renounce Christ and bow before the Roman emperor as a condition of release. When they refused, they were tortured and executed.

Eyewitness accounts from this time highlight the public brutality of the persecution. Believers were lashed until their muscles were laid bare, forced to lie down on shards of shells, and thrown into arenas to be devoured by wild animals in front of the townspeople. There are striking examples of early martyrs welcoming these sufferings in the name of Christ. One Germanicus even embraced the wild beast and pulled it toward himself to meet death as quickly as possible. But not all withstood the brutal torture. A man named Quintus, who had come forward of his own free will rather than wait to be arrested, when confronted with the beasts of prey, renounced Jesus and took the oath of fidelity to the emperor.

Though some bystanders wept with pity for the persecuted Christians, these spectacles of death and drama in the arena also served to sharpen the people's taste for Christian blood. Eventually the crowd took up the refrain, "Away with the atheists! Go find Polycarp!" ("Atheist" was a popular term for Christians, who in denying the Roman divinities in favor of a God who could not be seen, were thought of as atheists.)

Polycarp was undismayed by the growing public demand for his death. Rather than flee, the old bishop even resolved to remain in the city, where they could easily find him. His companions eventually convinced him to retreat to a farm outside of town, where the threat to his life was less immediate. There he spent his time in prayer, interceding for members of the church throughout the world.

Three days before his arrest, Polycarp fell into a deep trance. On regaining consciousness, he declared that he had received a vision. He had seen his pillow bursting into flame around his head. Polycarp had no question what the vision meant. Turning to his companions, he said, "I am going to be burned alive."

Not long after, the Roman authorities captured two slaves. One of them broke down under torture and revealed the location of the farm where Polycarp was staying. When soldiers arrived on horseback to seize him, Polycarp refused to run. Instead, he offered his captors hospitality and food, requesting only that he be allowed an hour for prayer. When they agreed, Polycarp prayed so earnestly that one hour became two, and several of the soldiers regretted their role in the arrest of such a venerable old man.

They then put Polycarp on a donkey and led him back into the city. Upon arrival, his captors ushered him into the carriage of a man named Herod, the captain of the local troops. Herod tried to convince Polycarp to save himself. "Why, what harm is there is saying, 'Caesar is Lord,' and offering incense?" When Polycarp refused the very suggestion of renouncing Christ, the official grew threatening and forced him out of the carriage so roughly that he injured his shin.

Without even turning, Polycarp marched on quickly as they escorted him to the stadium, where a deafening roar arose from the throngs of spectators. As he entered, his Christian companions heard a voice from above say, "Be strong, Polycarp, and play the man." He was brought before the proconsul, who urged him to deny his faith and bow before the emperor: "Swear by the spirit of Caesar! Repent, and say, 'Away with the atheists!'"

Turning with a grim look toward the crowd calling for his death, Polycarp gestured at them. "Away with the atheists," he said dryly.

Undeterred, the proconsul pressed him further to deny Christ. Polycarp declared, "Eighty-six years I have been his servant, and he has done me no wrong. How can I blaspheme my king who saved me?"

Once more the proconsul urged Polycarp to swear by Caesar. This time Polycarp replied, "Since you pretend not to know who and what I am, hear me declare with boldness: I am a Christian. And if you wish to learn more about Christianity, I will be happy to make an appointment."

Furious, the proconsul said, "Don't you know I have wild beasts waiting? I'll throw you to them unless you repent."

Polycarp answered, "Bring them on, then, for we are not accustomed to repent of what is good in order to adopt that which is evil."

Next the proconsul threatened to burn him alive. To this Polycarp replied, "You threaten me with fire which burns for a little while and is soon extinguished. You do not know the coming fire of judgment and eternal punishment reserved for the ungodly. What are you waiting for? Do what you wish."

The proconsul sent his herald out into the arena to announce that Polycarp had confessed to being a Christian. At this, the assembled crowd seethed with uncontrolled fury and called for Polycarp to be burned alive. Quickly, they assembled a pyre, gathering wood from workshops and the public baths. Polycarp removed his clothes and tried to take off his shoes, though his advanced age made it difficult. His guards prepared to nail him to the stake, but he told them calmly, "Leave me as I am, for the one who gives me strength to endure the fire will also give me strength to remain at the stake unmoved without being secured by nails." They bound his hands behind him. Polycarp offered a psalm of praise and thanksgiving to God. His captors ignited the wood.

According to observers, as the flames grew, they did not consume Polycarp as expected. The fire formed a circle around him, but his body did not burn. Since the fire did not have its intended effect on Polycarp's body, an executioner was ordered to stab him to death with a dagger. His blood extinguished the flames.

Observers that day were shocked by the contrast between Polycarp's martyrdom and the deaths of non-Christians they had witnessed. They beheld the same faithful discipleship in Polycarp's death that had characterized his life: a humble acceptance of God's will; praise of God in the most extreme trial; and a joyful, unwavering commitment to Christ even when faced with death.

Polycarp's was among the first recorded Christian martyrdoms. His steadfast obedience to Christ was a powerful testimony, an inspiration not only to the church he pastored so faithfully in Smyrna, but to Christians throughout the centuries.

3

Justin Martyr

died ca. 165, in Rome

AFTER THE DEATH of the last of Christ's apostles, a new era for Christianity began. As the faith spread across the Roman world, it met many challenges to its claims and practices.

Internally, heresies and cultic expressions began to confuse and divide the church, demanding response from its theologians. Externally, persecution – never far away for the early Christians – grew, the Roman Empire having outlawed the Christian religion. A key reason that the Roman government – typically tolerant of the diverse beliefs of its many conquered peoples – so despised Christians was the exclusive devotion of these men and women to the rustic Hebrew figure of Christ, whom they worshiped as the Son of God. Accustomed to pantheons of lesser and greater divinities, Rome might have better tolerated Christians if they had not refused to participate in the obligatory emperor worship – a required show of loyalty not just to a god but to the empire itself. Refusal to profess

13

Caesar as lord was seen as treason and prosecuted with torture and summary execution.

It was into this world that Justin was born, to a pagan, gentile family living in Flavia Neapolis (the biblical town of Shechem). His education left him unsatisfied, as his teachers failed to engage the bright boy's mind. Always curious about God, Justin bounced from one school to another, seeking answers to his questions with teachers from the refined Stoic, Aristotelian, Pythagorean, and Platonic philosophical traditions.

While Plato's ideas very much appealed to him, it was not until Justin met an old Christian man while walking near the beach (possibly at Ephesus) that he found the truth he was looking for. Their conversation convinced Justin that the ancient prophets were a more reliable source of truth than the philosophers. He changed the course of his life and study, giving his heart and well-trained mind to God. Traveling and teaching, he began to speak of Christianity as the "true philosophy." He adopted the traditional gown of a philosopher, eventually traveling to Rome, where he founded a small school after the custom of the classic philosophers.

This began a period of public work and teaching. Justin was an outspoken apologist for the faith, addressing his *First Apology* directly to the emperor in response to persecution of Christians. Well-versed in philosophy and comparative religions, he sparred with opponents both inside and outside the faith, refuting heresies and advocating for Christians in the wider public sphere. His position that "seeds of Christianity" predated Christ's incarnation allowed him to look favorably on elements of pagan thought that corresponded with or supported the tenets of Christianity, and thus he could refute the accusations of even the most educated of his pagan neighbors.

But his combative defense of the faith eventually made him enemies in the city. One of the philosophers he had argued with, a Cynic named Crescens, became a bitter enemy. According to Tatian, one of Justin's students, Crescens plotted against Justin and likely betrayed him to the authorities.

Whatever prompted their arrest, Justin and a group of his fellow Christians (likely his students) were captured and brought before the Roman prefect, Junius Rusticus. He addressed Justin, the obvious spokesman of the group. "Obey the gods at once," he demanded, "and submit to the emperors."

Justin, accustomed to defending his faith, replied immediately, "To obey the commands of our savior Jesus Christ is not worthy of blame or condemnation."

"What kinds of doctrines do you believe?" Rusticus asked.

"I have studied all faiths," Justin returned, "but I have believed in the true doctrines, those of the Christians – even though they do not please those who hold false opinions."

Rusticus felt the barb. "Are those the doctrines that please you, you utterly wretched man?"

"Yes," Justin replied.

"What do you believe?" the prefect asked again.

Justin answered, "We worship the God of the Christians, whom we believe to be one from the beginning, the maker and fashioner of the whole creation, visible and invisible, and the Lord Jesus Christ, the Son of God, who has been preached beforehand by the prophets as the herald of salvation. Since I am only a man, anything I can say is insignificant compared to his boundless divinity as the Son of God."

Rusticus questioned him further. "Where do you Christians meet?"

"Where each one chooses and can," Justin said, "Do you imagine we all meet in the same place? Not so – the God of the Christians is not limited by place, but being invisible, fills heaven and earth. He is worshiped and glorified everywhere by the faithful."

"Tell me where you assemble," Rusticus pressed, "or into what place you collect your followers."

"I live above a man named Martinus at the Timiotinian Bath," said Justin. "I don't know of any meeting in Rome other than this. If any wish to join me, I teach them the doctrines of truth."

"Are you not, then, a Christian?" Rusticus demanded.

"Yes," Justin said. "I am a Christian."

Justin's companions were also questioned, and gave steadfast witness to Christ. With their loyalties established, the prefect addressed Justin once again. "Listen, you who are called learned, you who think you know the truth. If you are scourged and beheaded, do you believe you will go up to heaven?"

Justin replied, "I hope that, if I endure those things, I shall have God's gifts. For I know that all who have lived faithfully will abide in his favor until the end of the world."

"You think you will ascend to receive some reward then?" Rusticus asked.

"I do not 'think' it, but I know and am fully persuaded of it," Justin declared.

"Then let us come to the point of the matter," the prefect continued. "You have come here together. Now sacrifice, with one accord, to the gods."

"No right-thinking person falls away from piety to impiety," Justin said.

"Unless you all obey, you will be mercilessly punished," Rusticus threatened.

"Through prayer," Justin replied, "we can be saved on account of our Lord Jesus Christ, even when we have been punished. This shall become salvation and confidence for us at another judgment seat – the more fearful and universal one of our Lord and Savior." The other Christians agreed with Justin's witness. "Do what you will," they said. "We are Christians and do not sacrifice to idols."

With this, the trial was concluded. Rusticus pronounced their sentence. "Let those who have refused to sacrifice to the gods and yield to the command of the emperor be scourged and led away to suffer the punishment of decapitation, according to the laws."

Justin and his companions were taken to the customary place of execution. In accordance with their sentence, they were beaten and then beheaded. Their fellow Christians secretly retrieved their bodies and gave them an honored burial as martyrs, rejoicing that their companions had remained faithful and inherited eternal life.

4

Agathonica, Papylus, and Carpus

died AD 165, in Pergamum
(Bergama in modern Turkey)

STANDING IN THE CROWDED STADIUM of Pergamum, a young woman named Agathonica watched as two of her fellow Christians, Papylus and Carpus, were dragged out for questioning.

The Roman proconsul in charge of the proceedings asked for Carpus's name. "My first and chosen name is Christian," Carpus replied. Flustered, the proconsul demanded that Carpus follow the orders of Caesar and sacrifice to the Roman gods. Carpus responded that the Roman gods were nothing more than "phantoms" and "demons," warning his interrogator that "they who sacrifice to them become like them."

"You must sacrifice," the proconsul continued. "The Caesar has commanded it."

Carpus replied that there was no reason to sacrifice to something dead: "They were never even men, nor did they ever live that they could die. Believe me, you are caught up in a grave delusion."

Turning to Papylus, the proconsul tried a different tactic. "Do you have any children?"

Papylus answered without hesitation, "Oh yes, many of them, through God."

An observer in the crowd called out: "He means he has children by his Christian faith."

Furious, the proconsul said, "You will sacrifice . . . or else! What do you say?" Like Carpus, Papylus refused.

Carpus and Papylus were hung up and flayed with instruments of torture. In spite of the torture, both held firmly to their faith. Seeing that they would never turn from Christ to worship the Roman deities, the proconsul decided to do away with them and ordered that they be burned at the stake. At this the guards nailed first Papylus and then Carpus to stakes, and burned them alive.

Agathonica was moved by the devotion of the two martyrs. She recognized God's glory in their actions and, though she was the mother of a young child, she felt called to step forward and join them. From the midst of the crowd she shouted, "This meal has been prepared for me. I must partake in it. I must receive the meal of glory."

Those around her begged her to remain silent, so as not to abandon her son. She replied, "My son has God who can care for him, for He is the provider for all. But I, why do I stand here?" She tore off her clothes and stepped forward to join the others in martyrdom.

As they had done with Papylus and Carpus, the Romans nailed Agathonica to a stake. Many in the crowd wept at the scene, and some began to cry out against the cruelty. But as her executioners set the wood ablaze, Agathonica shouted three times, "Lord, Lord, Lord, help me, for I fly to you." These were her last words.

5

Perpetua

died AD 203, in Carthage
(modern Tunisia)

PERPETUA, A YOUNG CHRISTIAN in the African city of
Carthage, was nearing the end of the time of training that every new
believer received. She and several other new believers – Saturninus,
Secundulus, Revocatus, and Felicitas – were preparing for baptism.
Their little group of disciples typified the diversity found within
the growing body of Christ. Perpetua was twenty-two, born to a
wealthy family, and the mother of an infant son. Revocatus and
Felicitas, who was pregnant, were both slaves.

But the group's Christian training was cut short when the
Roman authorities of the province arrested them for refusing to
worship the empire's deities. Though the current emperor was more
tolerant of Christians than many of his predecessors, there was still
widespread local persecution. Perpetua and her new friends were

imprisoned to await trial. She kept her baby with her. In solidarity, Saturus, another member of the group who had not been arrested with the others, turned himself in.

Soon after their arrest, Perpetua's father visited her. Knowing the danger to his daughter, he tried to convince her to turn away from her faith. She responded by pointing to some pottery in her cell. "Father, do you see this container lying here? Is it a little pitcher, or is it something else?"

"It's a pitcher," he replied.

Perpetua continued, "Can it be called by any name other than what it is?"

"No," he said.

Perpetua replied, "Neither can I call myself anything else than what I am – a Christian." Her father flew into a rage and attacked her physically. When he finally left, Perpetua gave thanks to God.

At this time, the prisoners were baptized in the prison and welcomed into the full community of the Christians. Perpetua's baptism was a deep source of encouragement for her.

Soon after, however, prison officials transferred the group to a worse section of the dungeon. Fearing for her baby in the dark, unhealthy environment, Perpetua asked her mother and brother to take him. Fortunately, it was soon arranged for the prisoners to be moved to a better part of the prison, where Perpetua could once again nurse and care for her child.

Perpetua's brother suggested that she ask God for a vision to discover the divine purpose of her captivity. Confident that she would receive one, she told him, "Tomorrow I will tell you." That night Perpetua saw an incredibly tall, narrow ladder made of gold and stretching to heaven. The ladder was beautiful except for one thing: all sorts of cruel weapons – swords, lances, hooks, and daggers – were attached to the sides of it, endangering reckless climbers. The weapons weren't the only danger; below the ladder she saw a huge, crouching dragon waiting to consume those who would not make the climb.

In the vision, Saturus made the climb first. Reaching the top, he encouraged Perpetua to join him. The dragon lifted its head as she approached, but undeterred, she stepped on its head as the first stride upward. She climbed the ladder and came to the top, where she found herself in an immense garden. A white-haired shepherd sat in the middle, milking his sheep. Around him were gathered thousands of people in white robes. The shepherd looked at Perpetua and said, "You are welcome, daughter." He offered her some cheese that he had made. She ate it, and the people looking on said, "Amen."

When Perpetua woke, she still tasted the indescribable flavor of the food she had eaten. After sharing the vision with her brother, they agreed that it meant she would end her time of imprisonment as a martyr.

Nearly worn out with anxiety, but having regained some measure of composure, Perpetua's father came again to visit her. "Have pity on your father," he said, "if I am worthy for you to call me father. Don't make me a subject of scorn. Think about your son too. He can't live without you." He kissed her hand, fell to the ground, and wept. Perpetua grieved too, but for a different reason. Out of her whole family, only he could not rejoice over her commitment to Christ. She was resolute. Again he left, taking her son with him.

The captives were brought to the town hall for public interrogation, and a crowd soon gathered. They were questioned one by one. When Perpetua's turn came, her father stepped to the front of the crowd, holding her infant son. "Have pity on your baby!" he cried.

The procurator in charge commanded Perpetua to "offer sacrifice for the well-being of the emperors."

"I will not," Perpetua answered.

"Are you a Christian?" he asked.

"I am," she replied.

The procurator ordered Perpetua's father to be beaten with rods, even though the elderly man had come to convince her to abandon Christianity. Perpetua watched, horrified, as the brutal command was carried out. Finally, the procurator condemned the prisoners to be thrown into an arena with wild beasts at the upcoming birthday celebration of the emperor's son.

After they were taken back to the dungeon, Perpetua asked for her child to remain with her in prison, but her father would not allow it. Perpetua noted that the child was weaned exceptionally quickly, easing her worry about leaving him behind. All to soon, the condemned Christians were transferred to a camp to await execution.

In the camp prison, the Christians found various ways to pass their final days. Perpetua chronicled their captivity in a diary, an account which would eventually be used to encourage others.

Pudens, one of the wardens overseeing the prisoners, grew fond of them, impressed by their courage in the face of torture and death. He allowed fellow Christians to visit them. These meetings refreshed and encouraged the prisoners. Not all of the visits were uplifting, though. Perpetua's father came again. He tore out chunks of his beard and threw himself on the ground in his grief for his daughter. To his surprise, she was not moved to save herself. Instead, she grieved for him.

In the days leading up to their execution, Secundulus died in prison. The others thanked God that he was spared a violent death. Felicitas was also expected to avoid the ordeal with the wild beasts, for she was now eight months pregnant and it was illegal to execute a pregnant woman. Yet far from being relieved, she was grieved that her pregnancy might prevent her from joining her companions in martyrdom.

Three days before the date of execution, Felicitas and the other prisoners joined in prayer. They begged God to grant her the privilege of facing the beasts with her fellow Christians, so that she would not have to face this trial alone later. She went into labor immediately. The early delivery was extremely painful. One of the servants attending the birth said, "You're suffering now – and what will you do when you're thrown to the beasts?"

Felicitas answered, "I suffer what I'm suffering now, but then there will be another in me, who will suffer for me, because I am about to suffer for Him." She gave birth to a girl. The baby was given to a Christian woman to be raised.

The day before their execution, Perpetua had a final vision. She saw Pomponius, a deacon who had visited her earlier, knocking at the gate of the prison. Perpetua went out and opened the gate for him, and saw that he wore a white robe. He said, "Perpetua, we are waiting for you; come!" He took her hand and led her through twisting tunnels and passageways until they came to the arena. They went out to the center. "Do not fear," he said, "I am here with you, laboring with you." Then he left.

The vision continued. Perpetua looked around at the great crowd in astonishment. The deadly animals were nowhere to be found. Instead, an Egyptian gladiator was to be her opponent. Then a giant man appeared, taller than the amphitheater. He called for silence and announced: "If this Egyptian should overcome this woman, he shall kill her with his sword; but if she shall conquer him, she shall receive this branch."

Perpetua and the Egyptian began striking one another. He grabbed her by the feet; she kicked him in the face. He lifted her in the air; she struck down toward him with her fists. Then she interlocked her fingers and brought down both her fists on him in one final blow. He crumpled. Perpetua stomped on his head. As the crowd cheered, she received the branch declaring her victory. When Perpetua awoke, she realized the meaning of the dream: her true battle would not be with the wild beasts, but with the devil. Though she might lose her life to the animals, she would triumph in the battle that mattered.

Finally, the day of the grim birthday celebration arrived. The Christians were led from the prison to the amphitheater, walking with joy in their hearts and on their faces. When instructed to put on the clothing worn by priests of the Roman deities Saturn and Ceres as part of the party's sick pageantry, they refused. The tribune overseeing the proceedings agreed that they could wear their own clothing. As they were led past the procurator who had condemned them, the Christians called out, "You have judged us, but God will judge you!" Because of this impertinence, the crowd demanded the Christians be scourged before the wild animals were released.

A bear, a leopard, and a wild boar were selected to face the men. When the boar was released, rather than attacking the captives, it turned and gored the huntsman who had brought it. The bear and the leopard attacked Saturninus and Revocatus. Saturus was taken out alone and tied to the ground near the bear, but the bear would not emerge from its den. Instead, the leopard (the animal Saturus had predicted would kill him) inflicted the fatal wound with a single bite. Calling to Pudens, the warden who was fond of the prisoners, the dying man said, "Farewell, and be mindful of my faith. Don't let these things disturb you, but confirm you." He asked that his ring be given to Pudens as a reminder of his death, and then he died.

The two young mothers were stripped naked and given nets to wear. Then they were thrown into the arena with a wild bull. Yet while the animal trampled and kicked at them, Perpetua seemed unconcerned with the brutal animal, carefully binding up her disheveled hair in order to meet death with as much dignity as possible.

After they had been brutalized by the animals, the surviving Christians were gathered together. They gave each other the kiss of peace one last time. Then each of them was stabbed with a sword.

But Perpetua, stabbed between the ribs by a novice gladiator whose hand was shaking, did not die. She cried out loudly, grabbed the gladiator's sword hand, and brought the blade to her own throat. In this way she embraced her death.

6

Tharacus, Probus, and Andronicus

died AD 290, in Cilicia (modern Turkey)

DURING THE PERSECUTION OF CHRISTIANS under the emperor Diocletian, three men were arrested and brought to trial before Numerius Maximus, the proconsul of Cilicia. Tharacus was a former soldier and a Roman citizen by birth, born in the city of Claudianopolis. Roman soldiers were required to take oaths and make sacrifices to Roman deities, so Tharacus had asked for, and been granted, a discharge from the army. Both Probus and Andronicus came from wealthy families.

Maximus asked for the men to be brought out one at a time for interrogation. When Tharacus was presented, Maximus asked his name. "I am a Christian," Tharacus replied.

Not a patient man, Maximus snapped at the guard, "Break his jaw and tell him not to answer me like that anymore!" He appealed to Tharacus further: "I want you, too, to be one of us who obey the commands of our lords, the emperors."

Tharacus countered, "But they make terrible mistakes; they are seduced by Satan." Maximus had the guards strike the prisoner across his cheek for suggesting that the emperors could err, but Tharacus was undeterred: "Yes, I said it, and I say it still: they are only men and are liable to make mistakes."

The proconsul commanded Tharacus to sacrifice to the Roman gods in a show of loyalty to the emperor, but he refused. Maximus had him beaten with rods. But between blows the prisoner said to him, "Truly, you have made me more prudent, since by these stripes you strengthen my confidence in God and his anointed Son, Jesus Christ."

Onlookers, undoubtedly disturbed by the brutality being inflicted on a citizen of Rome, were becoming uncomfortable with the proceedings. Demetrius, the centurion overseeing the beating, said to his victim, "O wretched man! Spare yourself! Follow my advice and sacrifice."

But Tharacus answered, "Leave, you servant of Satan, and take your advice with you!" Seeing that they were getting nowhere, Maximus ordered Tharacus back to prison in chains.

Next, the proconsul called for Probus. When Maximus asked his name, Probus answered, "My noblest name is Christian. People know me by the name of Probus."

Trying a gentler tack than he had with Tharacus, the proconsul said, "You won't benefit much by that name. Instead, listen to me and sacrifice to the gods. You will be honored by the princes and be our friend."

Probus responded, "I desire neither honor from emperors nor your friendship, for not small was the wealth I left behind in order to faithfully serve the living God."

Maximus had him stripped and placed in a rack, then tormented with raw thongs. Demetrius, the centurion, pleaded with him, "O wretched man! Look at how your blood spills out on the earth."

Probus answered, "My body is in your hands; but all these torments are a precious balm to me."

As he questioned Probus, Maximus called for more painful torture: "Flip him over and scourge his stomach. While you scourge him, ask him, 'Where is your helper?'"

But even as he was beaten, Probus answered, "He has helped me, and shall help me still." Maximus ordered him taken back to prison, and called for the third Christian.

When Demetrius brought Andronicus out, Maximus went through the same line of questioning. "What is your name?"

Andronicus replied, "You want to know who I am? I am a Christian."

The proconsul saw that this exchange would likely progress as the last two had. Still, he tried to deter Andronicus, saying, "Spare yourself, and listen to me as you would to your father. Those who have babbled such nonsense before you have gained nothing by it. Instead, honor the princes and the fathers, and be obedient to our gods."

Andronicus answered, "You were right to call them fathers; for you are of your father, the devil, and, having become one of his children, you're doing his work."

Maximus rejoined, "You are but a stripling. Will you despise and mock me? Do you know the tortures ready for you?"

"Do you think I'm a fool," Andronicus asked, "that I should be willing to be found inferior in suffering to my predecessors? I stand prepared to endure all your torments."

The proconsul had him racked, beaten on the mouth, and turned over to be tortured on his sides. All this time, Maximus continued questioning Andronicus, while Demetrius and the bystanders begged him to give in and end his suffering. Before sending him back to prison, Maximus ordered his men to scrape open Andronicus's wounds with broken bits of pottery. Afterwards, he was chained and taken away.

Some time passed. Unsatisfied with the outcome of his previous efforts, Maximus called the three men before him again, one by one, to be questioned and tortured. Tharacus was beaten on the mouth with stones until his teeth came out; his hands were burned with fire; he was hung up by his feet over thick, choking smoke; and vinegar and salt were poured into his nostrils. The other two prisoners suffered similar horrors as they were questioned. The three prisoners were then imprisoned separately so that they wouldn't be encouraged by seeing that their comrades had endured in faith.

One final time, Maximus had the three men brought before him. Each remained defiant. Tharacus was suspended, his jaw broken yet again, and his lips torn. His body was burned all over with hot irons. His head was shaved and hot coals poured onto the raw skin, until he screamed out, "May the Lord look down from heaven and judge!"

Maximus scoffed at him, "What lord do you call on, you cursed man?"

"The Lord you do not know," said Tharacus, "who pays back everyone according to their deeds."

Finally, the proconsul condemned Tharacus to be thrown to the wild animals. Not content to punish Tharacus only in life, Maximus added one last insult: "If you think your body will be embalmed by women, you're greatly mistaken. It is my intention that nothing shall remain of you."

As he was lead away, Tharacus replied, "Do what you please with my body, now and after my death."

Maximus hung Probus by his heels and branded him with hot irons on his sides, back, and legs. Probus said, "Your great power has not only made you a fool, but also blind, for you don't know what you are doing."

Maximus answered, "You have been tormented on your whole body except the eyes, and you dare to speak this way to me?" He turned to the torturers. "Pinch his eyes, that he may become blind."

Probus said, "Look, you have deprived me of my bodily eyes, but you shall never be permitted to destroy the eyes of my faith." At this, the proconsul condemned Probus to be thrown to the animals as Tharacus had been.

When Andronicus was brought forward, Maximus had his guards put flaming bundles of paper on his body. Andronicus said, "I may burn from head to foot, but the spirit is alive in me. You won't conquer me; the Lord whom I serve is with me."

Maximus ordered hot irons to be placed between Andronicus's fingers. He then ordered his men to force meat and wine sacrificed to the Roman gods into the prisoner's mouth. "See," mocked Maximus, "you have certainly eaten food sacrificed to the gods."

"Cursed be all who honor the idols," cried Andronicus, "you and your princes."

The proconsul said, "You degenerate – are you cursing the princes, who have given us such a lasting, tranquil peace? Put an iron into his mouth, break out all his teeth, and cut out his blasphemous tongue, that he may learn to no longer blaspheme the princes." After this, Andronicus could no longer answer Maximus's questioning. The proconsul condemned him to death.

The next day, a large crowd gathered in the Cilician amphitheater. Maximus presided over the public sacrifices. A group of Christians – friends of Tharacus, Probus, and Andronicus – hid among the crowd to observe the deaths of their brothers in the macabre festivities. When the proconsul ordered the three prisoners to be brought, the soldiers had to find people to carry the Christians out – the three men were so badly maimed from their torture that they could no longer walk. They were tossed like garbage in a heap in the middle of the arena.

When the crowd saw them, they became frightened. The people murmured to each other, shocked by Maximus's cruelty so visible on the bodies of the Christians. Many got up to leave. Maximus ordered his soldiers to note who in the crowd was leaving, so that he might question them later.

Then a bear and a lioness were released to devour the three men. The animals roared and thrashed about the arena so ferociously that the spectators were terrified in their seats. Yet the beasts would not go near the three martyrs.

Furious that he had been deprived of his show, Maximus ordered that the animals be slain. He ordered gladiators to kill the three Christians, then fight each other to the death. The gladiators entered the arena and stabbed Tharacus, Probus, and Andronicus to death where they lay.

After the killing, the Christians' bodies were tossed in a pile with the others who had died during the day's events so no one would be able to distinguish them from the pagan gladiators. Still, some fellow Christians managed to recover them, and gave them a proper burial, honoring their steadfastness and bravery.

7

Marcellus

*died AD 298, in Tingis
(modern Tangiers, Morocco)*

WHEN THE ROMAN SOLDIERS stationed in Tingis celebrated Emperor Maximian's birthday, one centurion by the name of Marcellus refused to participate.

It was not unusual for Christians to refuse to serve in the Roman army, pagan war machine that it was. Life as a Roman soldier did not lack for religious ceremonies, appeasing a pantheon of gods. Besides sharpening swords, a legionary must offer sacrifices and honor patron deities. The emperor, whose cult of divinity served to consolidate power over all strata of Roman society, was himself often the object of worship and prayer.

Nearly a century before Marcellus took his stand, Hippolytus, one of the earliest bishops of Rome, had addressed the requirements for soldiers who wished to become part of the Christian church. "A soldier of the civil authority must be taught not to kill, and to refuse to do so if he is commanded; also to refuse to take an oath. If he is unwilling to comply, he must be rejected."

Having recently become a Christian, Marcellus felt increasingly repelled as he watched his pagan army cohorts sacrifice to the Roman gods to honor the emperor. Finally, the moment of decision arrived. Marcellus stood up among those who had been his closest comrades, removed his belt and sword, and flung the insignia denoting his respected rank of officer to the ground. The other soldiers were horrified at this blatant desecration of the oath they had all taken when they joined the Roman army. They seized Marcellus and brought him before Fortunatus, the local governor.

When questioned, Marcellus spoke with the boldness of a man hardened by a soldier's life. "I tell you today, loudly and in public, before the standards of this legion, that I am a Christian and cannot observe any oath unless it be to Jesus Christ, the son of the living God." Fortunatus intended for Marcellus to make his case before the Emperor Maximian, who was known to be friendly to Christians. But instead, Marcellus was sent to stand trial before the prefect Agricolanus, a man with little mercy for Christians.

As the trial began, Agricolanus listened to an account of the actions and words of the accused. He asked Marcellus, "Did you do those things which are recorded in the governor's record?"

"I did," Marcellus responded.

"What madness possessed you to cast aside your oath and say such things?"

Marcellus countered, "No madness possesses him who fears God."

Confused, Agricolanus pressed Marcellus to explain his actions. The centurion answered at length:

> It is not proper for a Christian, one who fears the Lord Christ, to engage in earthly military service. What I have stated before to

the governor, Fortunatus, I now state before you. I am a Christian, and call only upon the true God and king, Jesus Christ, whom I love more than all the honor and riches of this world. By his law and command we are forbidden to take another person's life or even to bear arms. By his example we are taught to forgive those who harm us and to have mercy upon our enemies.

Those who call upon his name are children of peace, with no ill will toward anyone upon earth. Those who reflect the image of Christ know of no weapons other than patience, hope, and love – and these are only weapons to break the flinty hearts that have never been affected by the heavenly dew of the holy word. We know of no vengeance, however we may be wronged. We do not ask for vengeance, but with Christ we pray, "Father forgive them, for they know not what they do."

The prefect asked, "Do you not remember that you took your military oath, in rites over which all the gods presided, when you confessed the emperor's deity? Have you forgotten how you received the standards upon which the images of the gods themselves were placed for your protection?"

Marcellus said simply, "I will no longer sacrifice to gods and emperors, and I disdain to worship your wooden and stone gods, who are deaf and dumb idols. I serve Jesus Christ, the everlasting king! So far am I from seeking to escape suffering for the name of Christ, that I, on the contrary, consider it the highest honor which you can confer upon me."

His mind made up, Agricolanus stood and pronounced sentence. For rejecting his oath and refusing to sacrifice to the Roman gods, Marcellus would be executed immediately. The guards led away the soldier of Christ, and with a sword like that which he had once carried, cut off his head.

PART II

Radical Reformers

8

Jan Hus

died 1415, in Constance (modern Germany)

JAN HUS WAS BORN IN 1370 to a peasant family. He took his surname from the village of his birth, Husinec, in southern Bohemia (today a region of the Czech Republic). The word *hus* means "goose" in Czech, and later in his life Jan frequently used his name as a pun in his writings.

Although little is known of Jan's parents, his mother taught him to pray as a child, and encouraged him toward the priesthood as he grew up. This career path appealed to young Jan, not because he had much interest in the spiritual life, but because a priestly position meant significant wealth and prestige.

Though Jan's interests in religious matters quickly grew after he enrolled in the University of Prague, his selfish original motives were not unusual. He was born into a time of great unrest and complex political struggles within the Catholic Church, many of which centered on the priesthood.

The clergy of the day were known for immorality and corruption, accepting bribes, taking lovers in violation of their vows to celibacy, and practicing simony – the buying and selling of ecclesiastical positions. For example, in 1402 (the same year Jan was appointed preacher in the Bethlehem Chapel in Prague), a man named Zbyněk Zajíc purchased the archbishopric of the area for the considerable sum of 4,280 gulden, which paid off the debts of his two predecessors. Zbyněk was an ex-soldier, only twenty-five years old and lacking theological training of any kind. Though he originally got along with Jan, their congenial relationship was short-lived.

While at the University of Prague, Jan was influenced by the work of John Wycliffe, who had fought against the abuses of the Roman Catholic clergy in England. "Wycliffe, Wycliffe," Jan once wrote in a book's margins, "you will turn many heads."

The church owned about half of all the land in Bohemia, and the peasantry resented the heavy taxes that the clergy imposed on them. The people called for reform. Bethlehem Chapel, where Jan preached, became the heart of this movement. Following Wycliffe's lead, Jan began to speak out against clerical abuses. "They are drunks," he said of the priests, "whose bellies growl with great drinking and are gluttons whose stomachs are overfilled until their double chins hang down." He called them fornicators, parasites, money misers, and fat swine. "These priests," he said, "deserve to hang in hell."

He even speculated as to what Christ might say about the immorality of the clergy: "Everyone who passes by, pause and consider if there has been any sorrow like mine," Jan wrote in the voice of Jesus. "Clothed in these rags I weep while my priests go about in scarlet. I suffer great agony in a sweat of blood while they take delight in luxurious bathing. All through the night I am mocked and spat upon while they enjoy feasting and drunkenness. I groan upon the cross as they repose upon the softest beds."

For Archbishop Zbyněk, these accusations hit too close to home. He grew increasingly suspicious of Jan, and the two men became rivals.

At the time there were two competing popes, one based in Rome and the other in Avignon, France. Catholic nations were divided over which pope to follow. When the Council of Pisa was called in 1409 to settle the matter and reform the church, Jan was elated. Archbishop Zbyněk opposed the council, but Jan had King Václav IV of Bohemia (known as King Wenceslaus) on his side.

The Council of Pisa voted to depose both the Roman pope, Gregory XII, and his rival, Benedict XIII. In their place, the council elected Alexander V. But neither of the former popes submitted to the ruling of the council, so instead of two popes there were now three. Jan, believing Alexander V represented reform and progress, chose to acknowledge the new pope as legitimate. King Wenceslaus followed Jan's lead in supporting Alexander V, forcing Archbishop Zbyněk to do the same in order to stay in step with the king.

Zbyněk may not have been a spiritual man, but he was a cunning politician, with few scruples. He begged Alexander V to support his work prosecuting heresy, and sent the new pope a large bribe to ensure his support. After this, Alexander V issued a ruling prohibiting free preaching in private chapels. This gave the archbishop the pope's permission to censor Bethlehem Chapel.

But Jan Hus refused to obey the pope's orders. He continued his preaching and ministry in Bethlehem Chapel. Outraged, Zbyněk decided to destroy the chapel altogether. Jan described the attack: "Clad in armor, with crossbows, halberds, and swords, they attacked Bethlehem while I was preaching . . . wishing to pull it down, having conspired among themselves." But Jan had more than two thousand outraged worshipers on his side. Zbyněk's plan failed. King Wenceslaus, valuing Zbyněk's support, took no side in the matter.

Undeterred, Archbishop Zbyněk gathered more than two hundred copies of John Wycliffe's writings, brought them to the palace courtyard, and burned them to ashes. Jan condemned the archbishop's actions, saying, "I call it a poor business. Such bonfires never yet removed a single sin from the hearts of men. Fire does not consume truth. It is always the mark of a little mind that it vents its anger on inanimate objects. The books which have been burned are a loss to the whole people."

In response to the attack on the chapel and the book burning, the Bohemian people rioted, ridiculing Zbyněk on posters and in song, chanting: "Bishop Zbyněk, ABCD, burned books not knowing what was written in them!" The archbishop fled to his castle in Roudnice, and from its safety summarily excommunicated Jan – a severe punishment in a day when the church held huge influence in public life.

Still, Jan refused to stop preaching. He had the support of the people, but Zbyněk had the support of the pope. Persuaded by generous gifts from the archbishop, Alexander V issued another notice of excommunication. Jan ignored this one too. Then Zbyněk, emboldened by the pope's support, took the fight a step too far: he excommunicated royal officials in Prague, and in so doing incited the wrath of King Wenceslaus, who had stayed out of the conflict until this point.

When Jan was summoned to appear in Bologna as part of papal investigations into heresies, Wenceslaus replied, "If anyone wants to accuse Hus of any charges, let them do it here in our kingdom.... It does not seem right to give up this useful preacher to the discrimination of his enemies." Zbyněk hit back, pronouncing an interdict against the city of Prague, suspending all church activities – including marrying, burying, blessing, preaching, and administering communion.

With the support of his magistrates, King Wenceslaus demanded that Archbishop Zbyněk relent and cease all action against Jan Hus.

The king obtained a writ from Pope John XXIII (who replaced Alexander V after his sudden death) reversing his predecessor's actions against Jan. The king ordered Archbishop Zbyněk to make a public declaration clearing Jan of all heresy. But before the archbishop could follow orders, he died. According to old Czech annals, Zbyněk was poisoned by his cook – possibly a supporter of church reform.

With the archbishop's passing, it appeared Jan would be free from persecution. But then something happened that forced him to once again speak out against the church and the magistrates. In 1411 troops backing rival pope Gregory XII seized control of Rome. To pay for a counteroffensive, Pope John XXIII authorized the sale of indulgences – documents assuring forgiveness of sins swapped for cash by the clergy. King Wenceslaus, a supporter of Pope John XXIII, shared in the proceeds.

Many people in Bohemia viewed indulgences as yet another corruption of the money-grubbing clergy. Although he could have remained silent, Jan's conscience would not let him. He led the outcry against the sale of indulgences, calling for a boycott. He said he would not be persuaded to support indulgences "even if I should stand before the stake which has been prepared for me."

This brave action lost him the support of his greatest ally and protector, King Wenceslaus. Furious that he might lose the lucrative revenue stream generated by the sale of indulgences, the king said, "Hus, you are always making trouble for me. If those whose concern it is will not take care of you, I myself will burn you."

Jan remained defiant even in the face of the king's wrath, saying, "Shall I keep silent? God forbid! Woe is me, if I keep silent. It is better for me to die than not to oppose such wickedness, which would make me a participant in their guilt and hell." Jan was excommunicated a fourth time, and the city of Prague was, once again, placed under interdict. This time King Wenceslaus did nothing to stop it. For the sake of the city, Jan left Prague for the countryside, but he never ceased to preach or write.

In 1414, three men were still claiming the papacy, and there was no reconciliation in view. Sigismund, the king of Hungary and half-brother of King Wenceslaus, arranged for a new council to end the papal schism and eradicate heresy from the Western church. Sigismund invited as many magistrates and clergymen as he could. When all had arrived in the city of Constance, Germany, they formed the largest church council since the Council of Nicea in 325.

Jan Hus was among those invited. Sigismund personally promised Jan safe conduct. Despite the warnings of his friends, Jan believed him. When he arrived in Constance, he sent his friends a letter joking, "The goose is not yet cooked and is not afraid of being cooked." But a few weeks later, his enemies, hearing a rumor that Jan planned to flee the city, imprisoned him in the dungeon of a Dominican monastery. King Sigismund was furious that his promise of safe conduct had been breached, but the prelates who had imprisoned Jan convinced him that he was not bound to honor promises made to a heretic.

Pope John XXIII established a committee of three bishops to investigate the accusations against Jan. Jan was not allowed an advocate for his defense. The outlook was bad, and soon his situation worsened considerably. The Council of Constance voted to force Pope John XXIII and the other two popes to abdicate their positions. They said, "If anyone . . . including the pope, shall refuse to obey the commands, statutes, and ordinances of this holy council . . . he shall be subject to proper punishment." Pope John XXIII fled the city disguised as a laborer, and Jan was given over to King Sigismund.

The king now revealed his true beliefs about the "goose" from Bohemia. "I was but a boy," he said, "when this sect began and spread in Bohemia, and now look how strong it has already become."

Jan, chained at all times and poorly fed, became severely ill. Finally King Sigismund said, "There is enough evidence to condemn him. If he will not recant his errors, let him be burned." Though hundreds of Czech nobles signed petitions to free Jan at the Council of Constance, King Wenceslaus said nothing in his defense.

Jan suffered through a number of public trials, where excerpts from his writings were read and witnesses were called to speak against him. He was commanded to recant his heretical beliefs. Jan only replied that he would do so if his errors could be proved by scripture. He denied defending Wycliffe's more radical conclusions, but said that he could only wish his "soul might sometime attain unto that place where Wycliffe's is." At his final trial on June 8, 1415, thirty-nine sentences were read to him, all taken from his writing. Again, Jan said he would recant if anyone could prove his error using scripture.

But Jan's fate was already sealed. Any attempt he made to argue his case was drowned out by shouts from the attending clergy. One old Polish bishop cried out that the law was clear on how to deal with heretics. "Do not permit him to recant," another priest shouted. "Even if he does recant, he will not keep to it."

On July 6, 1415, Jan Hus was condemned to death before the council. He said to a friend that he would rather be burned publicly than killed in private, "in order that all Christendom might know what I said in the end." When Jan's books were condemned to be burned, he fell to his knees and prayed aloud for God to forgive his accusers.

He was dressed in his priestly vestments, but only as a mocking symbol – each piece was torn from him. As different bishops removed his stole, chasuble, and other vestments, they said, "O cursed Judas . . . we take from you the cup of redemption." They concluded by saying, "We commit your soul to the devil." A tall, paper miter such as a bishop would wear was placed on his head, bearing the image of three demons and the words, "The leader of a heretical movement." Guards ushered him away to the stake. A crowd of people followed.

At the stake, the executioner undressed Jan, tied his hands behind his back, and bound his neck to the stake with a chain. Wood and straw were then piled around him up to his neck. The imperial marshal asked Jan one final time to recant and save his life. Jan answered, "God is my witness that . . . the principal intention of my preaching and of all my other acts or writings was solely that I might turn people from sin. And in that truth of the gospel that I wrote, taught, and preached in accordance with the sayings and expositions of the holy doctors, I am willing gladly to die today." With that, the executioner started the fire.

According to some, the executioner had difficulty getting the fire going, which prolonged Jan's suffering. As the flames leapt higher, Jan cried out in agony, "Christ, son of the living God, have mercy on us!" From the roaring blaze he repeated those same words three times. Then he died. After the fire had subsided, his ashes were thrown into the Rhine River.

A hundred years later Martin Luther would ignite widespread church reform, influenced by the life and teachings of Jan Hus.

9

Michael and
Margaretha Sattler

died 1527, in Rottenburg, Germany

MICHAEL SATTLER was born in the town of Staufen, in the Breisgau region of southwest Germany. He was a hardworking student who grew into an intelligent, well-educated man. Eventually, he entered the Benedictine Monastery of St. Peter, near Freiburg. As he had in his studies, he excelled in monastic life, and eventually became prior.

But there were doubts and questions in Michael's mind that began to color his cloistered life. His study of the Bible, particularly Paul's letters, led him to question some tenets of Roman Catholicism. His uncertainty was compounded by the hypocrisy of other priests and monks in his community. While he took great pains to follow his monastic vows, other monks had mistresses.

Meanwhile, Reformation fervor was increasing across the Breisgau region. Michael's conscience was stirred by revolutionary peasants who occupied the monastery. His crisis of conviction came to a head. On May 12, 1525, he left the monastery in search of a new calling.

Some of the peasants occupying St. Peter's were Anabaptists. Their ideas impressed Michael, and he soon joined the movement. During his search for spiritual truth, he had learned the craft of weaving to support himself. In a final act of rebellion against his former monastic life, he married a woman named Margaretha.

Though little is known about Margaretha, it is reported that before marrying Michael she had been a Beguine, a member of a religious order of women who lived together like nuns and devoted themselves to caring for the poor and sick without taking life-time vows. One writer described her as "a talented, clever little woman." After their marriage, she and Michael earned their living by weaving cloth.

At this time, King Ferdinand I, whose holding included Breisgau, began his persecution, mercilessly suppressing any heresy against the Roman Catholic Church, but especially singling out Ana-baptists. Michael fled to Zürich in 1525 to join the Anabaptists there. He did not settle, but eventually returned to his hometown. Then, fleeing persecution again, he moved on to Strasbourg, and then to the Hohenberg territory in Württemberg.

Based out of the city of Horb, Michael soon gathered a sizable following. In February of 1527 he presided over a conference of Anabaptist leaders in Schleitheim to develop a shared statement of faith, as a foundation to unite Anabaptists in the region. Those present knew that further persecution awaited them, but Michael probably had no idea how immediate the danger was.

The authorities had discovered the Anabaptists of nearby Rottenburg, from whom they extracted information on those in Horb. When Michael set out from Schleitheim to return to Horb with the seven articles of his Schleitheim Confession in his coat, the government's men were ready for him.

When he and Margaretha arrived in Horb, they were arrested along with a number of others. The government seized the confession of faith he was carrying, along with descriptions of the church's plans and activities.

Michael had many supporters in Horb, and after his arrest the city officials feared an uprising. The prisoners were soon taken by Count Joachim von Zollern to the secluded town of Binsdorf. From his prison cell there, Michael wrote a passionate letter to his congregation in Horb, calling them to ardent faith and trust in God. He waited in prison with the others for three months while preparations were made for their trial.

Finally, twenty-four armed men moved the prisoners to Rottenburg for trial. A large panel of judges was presided over by the chairman of the court, Count von Zollern. An eloquent legal expert from Ensisheim, Eberhard Hofmann, was the most prominent prosecutor, pushing for the cruelest sentence possible. The mayor of Rottenburg, Jakob Halbmayer, was named as the attorney for the defense, but Michael declined his assistance, speaking for the group himself.

As the trial began, Count von Zollern listed the charges brought against the group. Seven applied to all nineteen of the prisoners, with Michael Sattler facing two additional charges. First, the group was accused of violating an imperial mandate (a reference to the Edict of Worms against Martin Luther in May 1521). Second, the Anabaptists were said to have rejected the presence of Christ in the bread and wine of the Eucharist. Third, the group was accused of rejecting infant baptism. Fourth, they were accused of rejecting extreme unction, the anointing of the sick or dying. Fifth, the prisoners were accused of despising Mary and the saints. Sixth, they refused to swear an oath to the governing authorities. Seventh, they were accused of breaking bread and taking it together with the wine in the same dish.

Michael was additionally charged with breaking his monastic vows by marrying Margaretha. He was also accused of teaching his followers to lay down their weapons and refuse to resist if the Turks ever invaded their country. Michael had said that he would rather fight against the persecutors who called themselves Christians, if war could be justified at all – an opinion that incensed the government. To those witnessing the trial, Michael's words made him more than a heretic; they made him a traitor to the empire.

Michael, speaking in defense of the prisoners, asked for the charges to be repeated so he could be sure to address their finer points. The clerk mocked him for this, saying to the judges, "Prudent, honorable, and wise sirs, he has boasted of the Holy Spirit. Now, if his boast is true, it seems to me, it is unnecessary to grant him this; for if he has the Holy Spirit, the same will tell him what has been done here."

Unshaken, Michael repeated, "You servants of God, I hope my request will not be denied; for the things you said are still unknown to me." This time, his request was granted.

After speaking with his companions, Michael addressed each accusation in turn. First, he refuted the charge that they had disobeyed an imperial mandate which forbade following Lutheran doctrine. Though the Catholics saw the Anabaptists as a Lutheran sect, they were not. Michael argued that they followed the gospel and the word of Christ alone. The other accusations he readily admitted to. The body and blood of Christ could not be present in the Eucharist because Christ was bodily present at the right hand of the Father, he argued. Baptism, Michael asserted, must be preceded by faith. As for the oil used in anointing the sick, he declared that the pope couldn't make the oil any better by blessing it. He denied the charge of despising Mary, only noting that she could not be our intercessor, for Christ is our sole mediator. He agreed that they had not sworn an oath to the governing authorities, for Jesus commanded his followers not to swear oaths. The seventh accusation, regarding taking the bread and wine from the same dish, he did not deem worthy of rebuttal.

As to the two charges made against him personally, Michael described how his study of scripture and his observation of the hypocritical monks and priests informed his decision to leave the monastic order. He explained, "When God called me to testify of his Word, and I had read Paul, and also considered the unchristian and dangerous state I was in; beholding the pomp, pride, greed, and great promiscuity of the monks and priests, I went and took a wife, according to the command of God."

Finally, he came to the last and, in the minds of his hearers, possibly the most damning accusation. "If the Turks should come," he said, "we should not resist them, for it is written: 'You shall not kill.'" Addressing his claim that if warring were right he would rather fight against Christians than Turks, Michael said, "You, who would be Christians, and who make your boast of Christ, persecute the pious witnesses of Christ, in the spirit of the Turks."

Michael denied that he or his companions had rebelled in any way against the government, or acted in any way against God or his Word. To truly test his theological claims, Michael suggested, the judges should bring theological experts to dispute his arguments using scripture alone. "If they prove to us with the Holy Scriptures that we are mistaken and in the wrong, we will gladly stop and recant, and also willingly suffer the sentence and punishment for what we have been accused of. But if no error is proven to us, I hope to God that you will be converted and receive instruction."

The judges found Michael's final remark preposterous. They burst out laughing. Hofmann, the prosecutor, answered, "You infamous, desperate villain and monk, shall we argue with you? The hangman will argue with you, I assure you."

Michael responded, "God's will be done."

Flustered by Michael's words, Hofmann snipped, "It would have been better if you had never been born."

Michael answered calmly, "God knows what is good."

At this, Hofmann became enraged, shouting, "You desperate villain and arch-heretic, I tell you, if there were no hangman here I would hang you myself and think that I had served God!"

The judges left to discuss the sentencing. Their decision must not have been quite as simple as Hofmann had supposed, for it took an hour and a half to determine the sentence. While they were away, the courtroom descended into chaos. Observers berated and mocked Michael. One of the guards jibed, "What did you expect for yourself and the others, that you have so seduced them?" Drawing his sword he said, "See, they'll argue with you with this." Michael remained silent. Another man asked why he had not "remained a lord in the convent," since Michael's high position in the monastery seemed far preferable to his current state. Michael answered, "According to the flesh I was a lord; but it is better this way."

The judges returned to the room. The observers fell silent to hear the sentence: "In the case of the Governor of His Imperial Majesty versus Michael Sattler, judgment is passed, that Michael Sattler shall be delivered to the executioner, who shall lead him to the place of execution, and cut out his tongue; then throw him upon a wagon, and there tear his body twice with red hot tongs; and after he has been brought outside the gate, he shall be torn five times in the same manner. Then burn his body to powder as a heretic."

As the prisoners were taken back to their cells, Michael spoke with Jakob Halbmayer, the mayor of Rottenburg, whom he considered responsible for the terrible conduct of the trial. He told the mayor, "You know that you and your fellow judges have condemned me contrary to justice and without proof. Therefore, take care and repent. If you do not, you and the others will be condemned to eternal fire in God's judgment."

On May 21, 1527, Michael was taken into the town marketplace. According to the sentence, the executioner cut out a large chunk of his tongue, but enough was left that observers could hear him pray for those torturing him. Using hot tongs, they tore two pieces of flesh from his body, then tied him to a ladder and threw him into a cart. On the mile-long journey to the site of his execution, the tongs were used to tear at his body five more times. Once again, he told the officials, the judges, and the people watching to repent and be converted. As the ladder he was tied to was hoisted up and placed into the fire, he prayed, "Almighty, eternal God, you are the way and the truth; since no one has been able to prove this as error, I shall with your help on this day testify to the truth and seal it with my blood."

The fire crawled slowly up his body, burning the ropes that bound his hands. Then, using a signal he had agreed on beforehand with fellow believers, Michael raised his hands above the flames, forefingers pointing to heaven, indicating that the pain was bearable and he remained firm in his faith. As death approached, he echoed his Lord's words, saying, "Father, into your hands I commend my spirit."

Three of the Anabaptists on trial with Michael were also executed. Others recanted and were banished from the country. Count von Zollern's wife attempted to convince Margaretha, Michael's wife, to recant her faith, but to no avail. The day after Michael's death, Margaretha was executed by drowning in the Neckar River – though she said she would rather have joined her husband in the fire.

Wolfgang Capito, an old host and friendly disputant of Michael's in Strasbourg, wrote to the council in the city of Horb to advocate for the Anabaptists still in prison. He also wrote the prisoners a letter of comfort. Although Capito was still wary of certain Anabaptist beliefs, he wrote of Michael, "He showed such great zeal for the honor of God and the church of Christ, which he would have pure and blameless and without reproach to those who are outside." Another leader, Martin Bucer, considered Michael a true martyr, despite theological differences. Bucer wrote, "We do not doubt that Michael Sattler, who was burned at Rottenburg, was a dear friend of God. . . . We have no doubt he was a martyr of Christ."

10

Weynken Claes

died 1527, in the Netherlands

THE DUTCH WIDOW WEYNKEN CLAES may have been a commoner by birth, but her bravery, faith, and conviction were anything but common. Weynken, a "Sacramentist" who became the first female Protestant martyr in the Netherlands, was not formally an Anabaptist (her death preceded the movement's arrival in Holland by a few years), but she held many beliefs that would later characterize Anabaptism, objecting to certain Catholic teachings and practices as unchristian and idolatrous.

Weynken's beliefs were put to the test when she was arrested by the Catholic magistrate. She was imprisoned in the castle of Woerden, then taken to The Hague to be arraigned before the Count of Hooghstraten and the Council of Holland.

A woman questioned Weynken in front of the gathered council. "If you do not turn from your errors," she warned, "you will be subjected to an intolerable death."

Weynken answered, "If power is given you from above to persecute me, I am ready to suffer."

"Do you not fear death," the woman asked, "which you have
never tasted?"

Weynken said, "I shall never taste death, for Christ says:
'Whoever keeps my word will never see death.' The rich man of
Christ's parable tasted death, and will taste it forever."

"What do you believe about the sacrament?"

"I believe your sacrament is made with flour, and if you believe
it is God, I say that it is your devil."

The woman questioning her continued, "What do you believe
concerning the saints?"

"I know no other mediator than Christ," answered Weynken.
When offered a confessor, she said, "I have Christ, to him I confess;
nevertheless, if I have offended any, I would willingly ask them to
forgive me."

After questioning, Weynken was taken back to prison. Monks,
priests, and even her closest friends visited her, trying to convince
her to take back what she had said before the council. One of her
visitors was a woman who said, "Dear mother, can't you think what
you please, but just keep it to yourself? Then you will not die." But
Weynken answered, "Dear sister, I am commanded to speak and
must do so; I cannot remain silent about it."

Weynken was visited by two Dominican friars, one to hear her
confession of sin, the other to instruct her in the faith. The second
man showed her a wooden crucifix. "See," he said, "here is your
Lord and your God."

Weynken replied, "This is not my God. The cross by which I
have been redeemed is a different one. This is a wooden god; throw
him into the fire and warm yourselves with him."

The other monk asked if she would like to receive the sacrament
on the morning of her execution. She said, "What God would you
give me? One that is perishable and sold for a penny?"

They asked, "What do you hold concerning the holy oil?"

She responded, "Oil is good for salad, or to oil your shoes with."

A few days later she was brought before the court again, where the Dean of Naeldwijck, the church inquisitor in charge of the case, read the verdict: "that she was found to be in error with regard to the sacrament, and that she immovably adhered to her views." She was declared a heretic and was given over to the secular branch of the government. However, the dean expressly stated that he did not consent to a death sentence. After the statements, he left the room with his two associates.

Immediately, however, the chancellor who now had jurisdiction over the case declared that she could not go without punishment, for her beliefs were a crime. The decision was announced: "She should be burned to ashes, and all her property confiscated." Hearing this, Weynken said, "Has all been done now? I beg you all, that if I have harmed or offended any, you will forgive me." A monk asked her if she feared her sentence. She replied, "No, for I know how I stand with my Lord."

On the scaffold where she was to be executed, she again asked for forgiveness for any offense that she may have caused the people. She smiled and approached her execution as if she were a bride walking down the aisle.

A monk asked her, "Will you not always and firmly cling to God?"

She said, "Yes, indeed."

The monk continued, "Now you will have to go into the fire; recant."

Weynken answered, "I am well content; the Lord's will must be done."

She went to the place where she was to be burned and stood confidently before the stake. As the executioner prepared the ropes he would use to strangle her in advance of burning, the monk asked, "Mother Weynken, will you gladly die as a Christian?"

She answered, "Yes, I will."

"Do you renounce all heresy?" he asked.

"I do," she said.

Finally, he said, "This is well. Are you also sorry that you have erred?"

With a final, deep breath, she said, "I formerly did err indeed, and for that I am sorry; this, however, is no error, but the true way. I cling to God."

She removed the scarf around her neck, and helped put the choke strap around her own throat. With that, the executioner strangled her. She calmly closed her eyes, and appeared to fall asleep.

William Tyndale

died 1536, at Vilvoorde (modern Belgium)

WILLIAM TYNDALE was born to a privileged family in the west of Gloucestershire, near the Welsh border of England. Little is known of his childhood, but he began a Bachelor of Arts degree at Oxford University in 1506. He graduated in 1512, became a subdeacon, and decided to pursue higher theological studies.

William received a Master of Arts from Oxford in 1515 and then spent four years at Cambridge University. Lutheran ideas flooded the halls of Cambridge at the time, and it is likely that this is where he developed his passion for reform. But as he pursued his studies, he lamented that his official coursework did not include the systematic study of scripture. He said of his teachers, "They have decided that no man shall look at scripture, until he is nursed by heathen learning for eight or nine years and armed with false principles, which clean shut him out of the understanding of scripture."

He left academia to join the household of Sir John Walsh at Little Sodbury Manor, north of Bath.

Between 1521 and 1523, William Tyndale served as chaplain to Walsh's household and tutored the family's children. From time to time abbots, deacons, and other clergymen visited to dine at Little Sodbury. William eagerly joined them in conversation about current events, particularly the work of Martin Luther and Desiderius Erasmus on the European continent.

During these conversations, he probed these spiritual leaders' knowledge of scripture. What he found shocked and disturbed him. He often disagreed with these supposed intellectuals of the church. Whenever this happened, he immediately opened the Bible to explain his position and refute their errors. Rarely could one of these clergymen keep up, let alone contend with him, in clear exposition of the Bible.

During one of these conversations, a member of the clergy, frustrated with William's reliance on scripture, said, "It's better to be without God's laws than the pope's."

"I defy the pope and all his laws," replied William, "and if God spares my life, before many years pass I will help the boy who drives a plow to know more of the scriptures than you do!"

Spurred by his dissatisfaction with the clergy's lack of appreciation for scripture and their growing disapproval of his teachings, William left the Walsh household in 1523. Before leaving he told John Walsh, "Sir, I see that I shall not be allowed to stay long in this country, and you will not be able, even though you are willing, to keep me out of the hands of the clergy. What things you'd suffer for keeping me, only God knows, and I would be very sorry for it."

William had a new personal mission: to translate the Bible, at the time nearly exclusively in Latin, into common English. He believed the Word of God should be available to all English people, no matter their place in the social hierarchy. John Wycliffe had created such a translation many years before, but his version was hand-copied and inaccurate – it was translated from the Latin Vulgate instead of the original Hebrew and Greek – and nearly unavailable. The church had banned unauthorized translations of the Bible since 1408.

Seeking to do things openly, William set out for London to receive ecclesiastical approval for his translation project. He hoped to use the Greek New Testament published by Erasmus – the first of its kind – for the project. And he had just the man in mind to approve his project: Bishop Cuthbert Tunstall. The London bishop was a well-known classicist who had worked with Erasmus on his Greek New Testament. William hoped to play off of Tunstall's friendship with Erasmus to convince him to approve his own translation project.

But when he approached Tunstall, the bishop declined, claiming that he had no room for William in his household. Taken aback by the excuse but undeterred, William preached and studied for a time in London, supported by a cloth merchant, Humphrey Monmouth. It wasn't long before he realized that "not only was there no room in my lord of London's palace to translate the New Testament, but there was no place to do it in all England."

In 1524 he left for Germany, never to return to England. He was deeply influenced by Martin Luther, who had been able to do German biblical translation work in Germany. William hoped for the same success in his project for English-speaking people. For the next year, he worked in Hamburg on his New Testament translation.

William worked directly from the original Hebrew and Greek, comparing his work to the Latin Vulgate and Luther's recent German translation. William's translation, of course, was explicitly illegal, against the church's decree. Only a few years before, in 1519, six men and a woman had been burned to death in England for nothing more than teaching their children the Lord's Prayer and a few other Bible texts in English rather than Latin.

William's facility and accuracy with the original languages were excellent, considering the difficulty in learning biblical Hebrew and Greek at the time of the Reformation. Very few scholars knew the languages, and William had used unusual study methods to master them. With the exception of the occasional public lecture, his Greek was essentially self-taught. His Hebrew, like that of a few other learned Christians of the Reformation, came from Jewish rabbis whom he studied under in Germany. The style of his translation was simple and beautiful, words suitable for the common people. His phrasing has had a tremendous influence on English translations and literature ever since.

In the beginnynge was the worde, reads his translation of the beginning of John, *and the worde was with God: and the worde was God. The same was in the beginnynge with God. All thinges were made by it and with out it was made nothinge that was made. In it was lyfe and the lyfe was the lyght of men and the lyght shyneth in the darcknes but the darcknes comprehended it not.*

He found a printer in Cologne named Peter Quentell who would produce his work, the first mechanically printed English translation of scripture. But Cologne was a dangerous place for anyone with Lutheran sympathies. When one of William's assistants let the content of his work slip out after drinking too much, Johann Dobneck, a staunch opponent of the Reformation, raided Quentell's press. Thankfully, William was warned. He escaped with the pages already printed.

William learned from his mistake. He looked for his next printer in Worms, a city in the process of adopting Lutheranism. As copies of his New Testament translation began to roll off the press, they were smuggled into England and Scotland. Six thousand copies were printed, but only two survive. The others fell into the hands of bishops who denounced William's work. Among these was Bishop Cuthbert Tunstall, whom William had approached for approval a few years earlier. Apparently there was a deeper reason why the bishop had rejected William than a full house. Tunstall warned booksellers not to carry the translation and even burned copies at St. Paul's Cathedral. A later scholar would note that this "spectacle of the scriptures being put to the torch . . . provoked controversy even among the faithful."

William Warham, the Archbishop of Canterbury, followed Tunstall's lead. He advertised that he was interested in purchasing any copies of William Tyndale's translation available. A friend of the translator, Augustine Packington, answered the archbishop's call, saying, "My lord, I can do more in this matter than most merchants that be here, if it be your pleasure. . . . I will assure you to have every book of them that is printed and unsold."

Warham answered, "Do your best, gentle master Packington! Get them for me, and I will pay whatever they cost; I mean to burn and destroy them all." Packington did precisely what he was told, selling any and all copies to the archbishop. Then he promptly delivered the proceeds to William, who used the money to improve upon his translation and print a second edition.

William Tyndale's work eventually made its way into the hands of King Henry VIII. The timing was excellent. The headstrong king had recently separated England from the Roman Catholic Church and declared himself head of the new church – all so he could divorce Catherine of Aragon, who had not provided Henry with a male heir. He immediately married Anne Boleyn, a "bewitching" young lady who had enchanted him.

But the majority of England mourned the separation from the Roman Catholic Church. Henry and his advisors began searching for ways to smooth things over with the public. Henry found his answer when his new wife showed him a copy of William Tyndale's 1534 edition of the English New Testament and a copy of *The Obedience of a Christian Man,* a book emphasizing obedience to governing authorities which William had written to answer critics who claimed reformation would fragment society and lead to rebellion against established rulers. After reading it, the king said, "This book is for me and all kings to read!" The ever-political Henry saw in William a potential master propagandist. He extended an invitation to William to return to England and write for the court.

But Henry's men discovered William to be different from what the king had imagined. Not only was William unwilling to leave his translation work (he was now busy translating the Old Testament), but he had previously argued from scripture that divorce was against God's will, specifically Henry's divorce of Catherine. He also had written that, to gain power, recent corrupt popes had manipulated naïve and foolish kings, including Henry.

When Henry was informed of these things, his admiration of William turned to disdain. The king's agents searched England and Europe with orders to kidnap the translator, but William was well hidden among the merchants in Antwerp. Eventually Henry gave up his search, but William had made an extremely dangerous enemy, and others would soon succeed where the king had failed to find him.

Henry Phillips, the disgraced son of a wealthy family, was desperate to improve his fortunes. After gambling his father's money away, Phillips had been branded a traitor and rebel. An English dignitary (probably Bishop John Stokesley, Cuthbert Tunstall's successor and an infamous opponent of reformation) approached Phillips, offering financial reward if he would spy on the English translator. Phillips agreed without hesitation.

In Antwerp, William was a guest of Thomas Poyntz, a relative of his previous benefactor, Lady Walsh of Little Sodbury. Henry Phillips gradually won the confidence of the English merchants of Antwerp, and eventually he befriended William. The translator invited Phillips to the Poyntz home, shared a meal with him, showed him his writings, and discussed the need for reform in England.

William trusted his new friend, but Thomas Poyntz had misgivings. He shared his suspicions with William, but the translator assured his host of Phillips' Lutheran sympathies. Thomas set aside his doubts.

Eager to make up for his initial mistrust, Thomas took Phillips on a tour of Antwerp. Phillips was full of questions about the alleys, buildings, and leadership of the town, and Thomas answered them all. Only later did Thomas realize that Phillips had been feeling him out to discover if, for the right price, Thomas might turn against William. Convinced he would not, Phillips left to take matters into his own hands.

After obtaining a small party of officers from Holy Roman Emperor Charles V's imperial court in Brussels, Phillips returned to Antwerp. Shortly after Phillips arrived, Thomas Poyntz left Antwerp on business in Barrow, eighteen miles away. Phillips took the opportunity to position the officers for an ambush. He convinced William to cancel his lunch plans and eat with him instead. Then, recognizing he was in a position to take further advantage of the trusting William, Phillips asked if the translator would lend him two pounds, claiming that he had lost his purse. William gladly gave Phillips the money.

On their way to lunch, the pair reached a narrow alley. William stepped aside to allow his friend through first, but Phillips politely insisted that William enter before him. Two officers entered the alley from the opposite direction, and Phillips – a much taller man than William – pointed down with his finger to indicate that this was the man they were supposed to arrest. The officers bound William's hands and delivered him to the castle of Vilvoorde, six miles north of Brussels.

Henry Phillips gained nothing by his betrayal. He spent the rest of his life fleeing the agents of King Henry. He traveled from Paris to London to Italy, stealing clothes from friends and begging his family for help. Eventually, he was captured and given a choice between losing his eyes or his life. Nothing is known of miserable

Phillips' fate beyond this point, though one account envisions him "consumed at last with lice."

William Tyndale, imprisoned in the dungeons of Vilvoorde, resigned himself to his fate. Thomas Poyntz and other friends (including King Henry's own chancellor, Thomas Cromwell) did everything they could to help William, to no avail. Poyntz's efforts resulted in his banishment from the Low Countries, the loss of his merchant interests, and separation from his wife and family for years.

Though he suffered from cold day and night, William did not let his time in prison go to waste. Knowing what likely awaited him at the end of his captivity, he poured himself into writing one final treatise, *Faith Alone Justifies before God*, a summary of the gospel. Through the winter, he only had a few hours of daylight to work. During the long nights, he could only sit and wait in silence for the sun to once again shine into his cell. The only letter written by William's own hand that survives to this day is a plea to the prison governor for a few essential items to help in his study: warmer clothes, his Hebrew Bible, his Hebrew grammar, and his Hebrew dictionary.

Finally, after he had been eighteen months in prison, William's trial began. Gaunt from insufficient food, he was brought before his judges and a crowd of spectators. The presiding judge silenced the assembly and said, "He has been arrested for many great heresies; his chamber has been searched, and prohibited books have been found in great numbers; and he has himself composed many treatises containing heretical opinions, which have been widely circulated."

His charges were read before the assembly:

First, he maintains that faith alone justifies.

Second, he maintains that to believe in the forgiveness of sins, and to embrace the mercy offered in the gospel, is enough for salvation.

Third, he avers that human traditions cannot bind the conscience, except where their neglect might occasion scandal.

Fourth, he denies the freedom of the will.

Fifth, he denies that there is any purgatory.

Sixth, he affirms that neither the Virgin nor the saints pray for us in their own person.

Seventh, he asserts that neither the Virgin nor the saints should be invoked by us.

Many similar charges followed, though in reality his main offense had been translating the Bible. In August 1536 he was condemned as a heretic and sentenced to death.

Before a large crowd of clergymen, William was defrocked. He was led out in his priestly vestments and forced to kneel before his accusers. His hands were scraped with a knife or a piece of glass to symbolize the removal of his anointing with oil. Bread and wine of the Mass were placed in his hands, then immediately taken away. Finally, his vestments were torn from him one by one and replaced with the clothes of a layperson.

Two months later, in October 1536, the date of his execution came. William Tyndale was taken outside the city to the place of execution – a large pillar of wood surrounded by a circle of stakes. He was ordered one final time to recant. According to John Foxe, who recounted William's story in his *Book of Martyrs* in 1563, William said nothing for some time, then uttered a few final words: "Lord, open the King of England's eyes."

With that, the executioner bound William to the stake and fastened an iron chain around his neck. Above that, a hemp noose was tightened at his throat; he was to be strangled before being burned.

After brushwood and logs had been piled around William, the executioner pulled back on the noose. Before long, William no longer drew breath. The pyre was engulfed in flames, and William's body burned with the wood.

Three years later, William's prayer that the King of England's eyes would be opened was answered. In 1539, at the encouragement of his chancellor, Thomas Cromwell, Henry VIII required every church in England to provide its parishioners with a copy of the English Bible compiled by Miles Coverdale, largely translated by William Tyndale. A recent analysis of the 1611 King James Version of the Bible estimates that William's translation accounts for 76 percent of its Old Testament and 83 percent of its New Testament. As William had once dreamed would happen, the English Bible was finally in the hands of the plowboy.

12

Jakob and Katharina Hutter

Jakob died 1536, in Innsbruck, Austria, and
Katharina in 1538, in Schöneck (modern Italy)

IT IS NOT KNOWN WHEN JAKOB HUTTER, a hat maker from the rugged Alpine valleys of Tyrol who may well have taken part in the peasants' revolt of 1925, first encountered the nonviolent teachings of the "dangerous" Anabaptists. The Anabaptists taught that the Roman Catholic Church had strayed from the original teachings of Christ. Their rejection of infant baptism, and promotion of adult baptism as a sign of voluntary discipleship, quickly made them a target of fierce persecution, not only from the Catholic Church but from Protestant groups as well.

Embracing the Anabaptist teachings with conviction, Jakob Hutter became a zealous convert. After Georg Blaurock, the last of the founders of the movement, was burned at the stake in September 1529, Jakob spearheaded the mission in Tyrol, teaching, baptizing, and helping new believers form Anabaptist congregations. In 1531 he baptized Katharina Purst, a young servant girl who later became his wife.

With Jakob's entrance into ministry, Anabaptist groups in Tyrol found a leader to galvanize them in the face of growing persecution. His leadership and his emphasis on the communal nature of the church began to unite the growing movement. Converts pooled their money and possessions in a common treasury, in keeping with the early Christians' example. Although his accusers would later claim that he baptized for money, the common purse drew groups of Anabaptist believers closely together and provided for those in need.

The ruling powers now felt threatened not just by new religious teachings, but by this radical economic model of sharing. Travelling and teaching throughout the Tyrol region, Jakob quickly drew their attention. Ferdinand I, the king of Bohemia, Hungary, and Croatia, was openly antagonistic toward this upstart movement of "heretics," whose beliefs challenged the cozy marriage of the Catholic Church and the state. A pious Catholic, Ferdinand considered himself a defender of the faith against the growing number of Protestants in his land, in particular the widely-hated Anabaptists. In one report to Ferdinand, it was said of the Anabaptists that "more than seven hundred persons have been in part executed, in part expelled, in part have fled into misery, who left their property as well as their children behind."

Moravia (in today's Czech Republic) had a tradition of religious tolerance, and Anabaptists from all over Europe were converging there. The church in Tyrol sent Jakob with a companion to find out what the situation there was. He was thrilled to find believers living together in full community in the town of Austerlitz. The *Chronicle,* an early history of the movement, reports: "They found that both groups were of one heart and soul in serving and fearing God. Thereupon Jakob [and his] companions, in the name of the whole church, united in peace with the church at Austerlitz." They then returned to the work in Tyrol.

By 1533, the intense persecution had made it nearly impossible for Anabaptists to remain in Tyrol. Communities were being spied on, betrayed, hunted down, and seized by the police. Jakob Hutter was particularly targeted for his zealous missionary activity, but he managed to evade the authorities. The clergy worked hand in glove with government officials. As one account put it, "The priests, too, thundered from their pulpits that the people should watch out for them, seize them, and destroy them by fire and the sword."

The authorities turned people against one another, promising informers monetary rewards. Spying became rampant. More and more Anabaptists fled to Moravia. Some made it without major incident, but many were arrested along the way, tortured, and sometimes executed. Jakob heard reports of some believers whose cheeks had been burned through before being released. One immigrant, Peter Voit, was captured and imprisoned in Eggenburg. His jailers clamped his legs so tightly in the stocks that gangrene set in. Voit watched in horror as mice took the toes from his feet. When he was finally released, both his legs had to be amputated. Despite these afflictions, Voit survived the persecution and lived to an old age.

Jakob Hutter returned to Moravia in August 1533. Here he encountered opposition from within the movement as well as from without, as some of the leaders resisted his spiritual authority. They slandered Jakob's followers, even refusing to eat with them or greet them in passing on the street. But Jakob was able to expose the lies and eventually lead the diverse group to become a unified church.

Meanwhile, the city of Münster was taken over by a fanatical branch of Anabaptism under a tailor from Holland named Jan van Leyden. Like Jakob Hutter, he used scripture to argue that only adult believers should be baptized and established community of goods. But while other Anabaptists refused to use physical violence, even in self-defense, the followers of Jan van Leyden had no such qualms. They drove out citizens of Münster who would not be rebaptized and seized control of the city government. However, Münster was soon retaken, and van Leyden was captured along with two of his companions. The three were tortured with hot tongs and then executed, their bodies hung in iron baskets from the highest tower in Münster.

King Ferdinand used this revolution as a pretext to drive the Anabaptists from Moravia. Though they denied any connection with the Münsterites and condemned their actions and practices, the local authorities conflated the two groups, and many were imprisoned and tortured. In 1535, Moravia granted Ferdinand's request and banned all Anabaptists from the country.

Meanwhile, Jakob's group had decided to stop working as laborers in any way that benefited the Catholic Church, viewing such actions as funding idolatry. When they refused to work the vineyards of an abbess who had let them settle on her lands in Auspitz, she was outraged and forcibly evicted them. Due to Ferdinand's decree, they could find nowhere to settle and were forced into a nomadic lifestyle, wandering through fields and hills.

At one encampment someone reported them to the authorities, accusing them of carrying weapons. When the governor's men reached the camp they found no weapons, but many children and sick people. Jakob explained their situation, pleading with them to leave his followers alone. The deputation told him that he needed to make his case to the governor in writing. But when the governor received Jakob's strongly worded letter, he directed his servants to immediately return and arrest him. Although Jakob once again escaped, two of the group were arrested, racked, burned, and questioned under torture about money and supplies their group was thought to be hiding. One of them recanted under torture. The other was burned alive.

After this, the community decided that it was no longer safe for Jakob to remain with them. They unanimously voted that he should return to Tyrol to gather the remaining Anabaptists. Before he left, he placed a man named Hans Amon in charge of the group. Then, Jakob and his wife, Katharina, began the dangerous journey back to the Tyrol.

Jakob wrote several letters to the church in Moravia, encouraging them and telling them of his work in Tyrol, where he taught and baptized despite intense persecution. In his final letter, Jakob wrote, "In our hearts there is great pain and sorrow for your sake, and outwardly we, too, are suffering severe persecution. The horrible, raging dragon has opened its jaws wide to devour the woman robed with the sun, who is the church and the bride of Jesus Christ."

Finally, on November 29, 1535, Jakob and Katharina were captured and the two were separated, never to see each other again in life. Jakob was gagged and taken to the city of Innsbruck, where King Ferdinand's government resided.

Though a theologian was brought in to try to convert Jakob and prove him wrong with scripture, his attempts were fruitless. Jakob adhered steadfastly to his Anabaptist beliefs. Besides, King Ferdinand had already declared that, "Even if Hutter should renounce his error, we will not pardon him, for he has misled far too many; but we will let the penalty which he has merited so abundantly take its course." Jakob's fate was sealed.

They put him in ice-cold water, then took him into a sweltering room and beat him with rods. His captors slashed his body, poured brandy into his cuts, and then set the alcohol on fire. To stop his incessant proclamations against them, they gagged him. Perhaps as a mockery of his original trade as a hatter, they placed an outlandish hat on his head to humiliate him.

The court feared that he would be perceived as a hero if he were executed publicly, so they recommended killing him by sword at dawn, when the city would be most quiet. But King Ferdinand demanded a public execution as an example for others. On February 25, 1536 Jakob Hutter was burned at the stake in Innsbruck. "Come closer, those of you who contradict me!" he called out. "Let us test our faith in the fire. This fire will harm my soul as little as the fiery furnace harmed Shadrach, Meshach, and Abednego."

According to an official report, Katharina persisted "in her obstinate foolish opinion." She was transferred in captivity to the town of Gufidaun, and as with Jakob, a man was assigned to convert her. However, security was lax – likely because she was pregnant – and she escaped before the man arrived. Katharina continued her martyred husband's work for two more years, until she was finally arrested again. This time she was executed immediately, by a "third baptism," as drownings of Anabaptists were mockingly dubbed by the state.

After his death, Jakob Hutter was mourned and revered by his followers, who preserved his teachings and remembered his life in song. Hans Amon, the man Jakob had left in charge of the Moravian congregation, said that Jakob "gave a great sermon through his death, for God was with him." Although many of his detractors continued denouncing him even in death, one of his former opponents testified, "No one provided so faithfully for the people in temporal or spiritual matters as Hutter. Never was he found unfaithful. Through him the Lord gathered and preserved his people." Even though Jakob Hutter led them for just three short years, the Hutterite communities that still bear his name today keep alive the witness of this bold hat maker from Tyrol.

13

Anna Janz

died 1539, in Rotterdam, the Netherlands

A GIRL NAMED ANNA was born to a wealthy family in Briel, a town in South Holland. Little is known of her life until she married a man named Arent Janz. The couple was baptized in 1534, when Anna was twenty-four, by a Münsterite named Maynart von Emden.

Anna's story highlights the complexity of Anabaptism at the time. Von Emden was proclaiming the arrival of the New Jerusalem in the city of Münster, a common refrain at the time among those influenced by the apocalyptic teachings of Lutheran preacher Melchior Hoffman. Some restless leaders, hungry for revolution, took Hoffman's teachings as a directive to prepare the way for the return of Christ. But even though they used scripture to support their position, their way was anything but that of the peaceable kingdom. The group took over Münster's government, abolished private property, redistributed the wealth of the city's citizens to the poor, and made adult baptism a requirement for all residents.

Maynart von Emden was spreading the news and teachings of this group when he baptized Anna and her husband. At the time, encouraged by the successful takeover of Münster, a similar group of revolutionaries began marching in the streets of Amsterdam, proclaiming "the day of the Lord." They hoped to follow the example of Münster, raising a militia of armed citizens large enough to overthrow the city government. The authorities responded by arresting Anabaptists across Holland, whether or not they had been radicalized by the extreme teachings of this group.

When the hunt for Anabaptists came to Briel, Anna's husband fled to England. She stayed behind. She had met an Anabaptist leader named David Joris, a rival of Menno Simons. Joris opposed Simons's emphasis on a Bible-centered church, teaching that mystical revelations held greater authority than scripture. But, like Menno Simons, he championed nonresistance over the violence used by the Münsterites. His teaching on nonviolence captured Anna's heart.

Under the leadership of Joris, Anna realized that she could prepare for the arrival of the New Jerusalem without resorting to the mad violence of the Münsterites. Earlier she had written a song called "The Trumpet Song," which became a favorite of Anabaptist activists. In it, she hailed God's vengeance and justice, anticipating the day when true believers would "wash their feet in the blood of the godless." Now Anna supported Joris in his nonviolent leadership, and the two became close friends and confidants. She called him a "valiant leader of Israel" and urged him to "prepare the Lord an acceptable people, so that he may speedily come into his temple."

Her close relationship with Joris troubled her husband, Arent, who feared that she had committed adultery or would soon. He returned from England to confront her, and brought her back to

England with him. Their stay in England was to be short, though. Two years after their arrival, Thomas Cromwell initiated a new wave of persecution against Anabaptists in England, forcing Anna to return to the Netherlands. She was accompanied by her fifteen-month-old son, Isaiah, and an older female companion named Christina Barents. The historical record does not reveal what happened to Arent, but he was likely a victim of the persecution that drove Anna and their child back to their homeland.

Soon after returning to Holland, Anna and Christina were arrested. While they had been traveling, someone on the road had heard the two women singing an Anabaptist song and reported them to the authorities. In prison, Anna composed a letter to her son, reminding him of God's solidarity with the poor and the weak, calling him to follow her along the path of faithful suffering blazed by Jesus Christ, and encouraging him to live simply and generously.

Anna was sentenced to death in Rotterdam for her beliefs. When the time came for her execution, Anna's thoughts were on her son. She cried out to the crowd gathered to watch her die, offering her significant fortune to anyone willing to raise her boy. A baker accepted her offer, taking her son and the testament she had written for him in prison.

"Behold," she wrote to Isaiah, "I go the way of the prophets, apostles, and martyrs, and drink of the cup of which they all have drunk. I go the way which Christ Jesus – the eternal Word of the Father, full of grace and truth, the shepherd of the sheep, who is the life – himself went. . . . See, my son, this way has no retreats; there are no roundabout or crooked little paths; whoever departs to the right or to the left inherits death. . . . There are some who well perceive that this is the way to life, but it is too severe for them; it pains their flesh. . . . May the Lord cause you to grow up in his fear, and fill your understanding with his spirit. Sanctify yourself to the Lord, my son."

Anna and her companion, Christina, were drowned at nine in the morning on January 24, 1539. The letter she wrote to her son was preserved by her fellow believers, giving strong expression to her faith in the face of persecution and her deep commitment to walking with God in peace and the light of the Bible. The baker who took in her son increased in prosperity, and Isaiah eventually became mayor of Rotterdam, the city where his mother had been put to death.

14

Dirk Willems

died 1569 in Asperen, the Netherlands

AS DIRK WILLEMS FLED across the frozen Linge River, he heard ice breaking behind him. He turned around and saw that the policeman pursuing him had fallen through. So without hesitating he ran back and pulled the man from the frigid water. It was, to him, as natural as eating and drinking.

Once they reached the shore, the rescued man urged Dirk to flee. But the officer's superior arrived on the scene and yelled, "Remember your oath!" So the policeman whom Dirk had saved took him captive, knowing there wasn't much chance that Dirk could escape death now.

At Dirk's sentencing, one of the seven judges read out the charges against him. It was a classic case of Anabaptist heresy. He had been rebaptized as a teenager. He had, at his house, hosted secret meetings where prohibited doctrines were taught. Worst of all, he had allowed several people to be rebaptized in his home. This was "contrary to our holy Christian faith," the judges asserted, and ought to be severely punished.

The decree said that he was to be "executed with fire until death ensued." Those who watched Dirk die remembered how sickening the experience was, and yet how steadfast he remained. He was burned at the stake outside Asperen. A strong east wind was blowing that day. It blew the flames away from his upper body, making his death all the more painful. But through it all, he repeatedly called on God, so loudly that people downwind in the nearby town of Leerdam could hear his voice.

Remorse filled one of the judges as he watched Dirk die. Eyewitnesses reported that this judge couldn't bear Dirk's suffering in his final moments and ordered the executioner to do something to hasten his death.

Today the *Martyrs Mirror* engraving of Dirk Willems turning around to save the life of his pursuer has become a symbol of Anabaptism and its commitment to loving one's enemy and returning good for evil. Dirk is remembered all over the world, not just for his courage but for his simple obedience to Jesus' commands to "do to others what you would have them do to you," and to "bless those who persecute you."

PART III

Early Modern Witnesses

15

Veronika Löhans

persecuted 1738, on St. Thomas
(Virgin Islands)

VERONIKA LÖHANS STRUGGLED to understand an Afro-Caribbean man speaking to the crowd. Far back, under a palm thatch roof without walls, she watched the light of a lantern on his face. The man spoke eagerly, in short syllables. He was tall and strong and moved his arms quickly. Veronika smiled to herself in the dark. Even though she did not understand everything he said, she did not fear him as she would have as a child. She loved him, a brother in the church community, and to see how he spoke to the people made her glad.

Mosquitos swarmed about. Like the other women at the meeting, Veronika slapped them from her legs and waved them from her ears. She wondered how the men, mostly without shirts, could ignore them so well. But glancing around her, she saw that no night-flying bugs would disrupt the eager attention of this crowd.

Faces kept emerging from the darkness under low-hanging coconut palms. More and more – perhaps over five hundred faces – surrounded the light and kept drawing closer to hear what was said. In spite of the humidity and bugs, in spite of the ever-tightening crowd, Veronika felt deeply thankful for having come to St. Thomas in the West Indies. The Savior was present here, and with the seekers around her, she found joy in coming together to worship him.

Veronika was young – only married a few months – but the road behind her was already long. A peasant girl from the backwoods of Moravia, she had spent a year in prison for having attended secret meetings of believers. On her release, she had fled through the mountains of Silesia to Germany. There she had joined the congregation of believers at Herrnhut in Upper Lusatia, on the lands of Count Nikolaus Ludwig von Zinzendorf, who had become one of their own and a leader among them.

Immediately after her marriage to Valentin Löhans in 1738, the community at Herrnhut had agreed to send them out as missionaries to the New World. They traveled overland to Rotterdam, and from there they set sail for the island of St. Thomas.

Now Veronika sat among believers on the Posaunenberg, where on a twenty-seven-acre lot the brothers had built houses among flowering jasmine and lemon trees. In the crowd gathered there to worship she saw few white faces – until a sudden commotion turned all heads.

Rough men with swords and whips charged in on the multitude. Roars and shouts drowned out the screams of terrified children. "Kill them! Shoot them! Beat them! Stab them!" Veronika distinguished the white men's crude voices at once from the musical West Indian patois, and they struck terror to her soul.

Benches rolled over as desperate mothers around her snatched their children to flee. Swinging cutlasses, heavy-booted men smelling of cane liquor charged into the circle of light beneath the lantern. They caught the one who had been speaking – a brother baptized "Abraham" – and began to beat him wildly. One white man hit a woman over the head as she tried to shelter her baby. She clutched her child tighter while another man cracked a bull whip around her. Elisabeth Weber, a European sister, was stabbed through the breast, and a cutlass sank deep into Veronika's shoulder.

Within minutes the multitude had vanished into the surrounding darkness, the intruders had galloped off on horseback, and only the severely injured lay groaning among patches of blood on the hard-packed earth. When the coast was clear, the sugar cane rustled and a few of the brothers returned.

At the scene of violence they knelt to pray for their white Protestant persecutors. Some prayed in the West Indian dialect and some in the languages of central Europe. Abraham, the strong young man who did not retaliate when the drunks beat him, prayed with tears for their "awakening."

Within three weeks of the attack, the church community on St. Thomas (consisting almost entirely of black slaves owned by white "Christian" slave owners) sent out sixteen missionaries. They reached every plantation on the island and the number of believers increased so rapidly that landowners threatened to leave unless the governor crushed the movement at once.

What brought a great company of Africans and Europeans into previously unheard of unity in the Caribbean? What inspired young peasant women to cross the ocean and brave life in strange tropical lands where everyone predicted they would die?

It started when Zinzendorf and David Nitschmann travelled from Herrnhut to Copenhagen. There, in the home of a Danish nobleman, they met Anton Ulrich, a black slave from the West Indian island of St. Thomas. The brothers listened, spellbound, as Anton told of slave transport to the New World, their wretchedness on plantations there, and how he used to sit on the shore of St. Thomas longing to know God.

After baptizing Anton at Copenhagen, Zinzendorf brought him back to Herrnhut, where he spoke to the whole congregation on July 21, 1731. In halting Danish, with gestures and stories that struck the believers to the heart, Anton described slavery. "But to speak to my people would be difficult," he told them. "To reach them you would most likely have to become slaves yourselves."

That night after the meeting, Johann Leonhard Dober, a young potter who had come to Herrnhut from Silesia, tossed and turned in bed. The thought of innumerable people living and dying in bondage, without hope and without knowing God, kept him awake until morning. The next day he wrote to the congregation offering to go to the West Indies:

> I can tell you that my intention has never been just to travel abroad for a while. What I desire is to dedicate myself more firmly to our Savior. Ever since the count has returned from Denmark and spoken of the condition of the slaves, I have not been able to forget them. So I decided that if another brother would like to accompany me, I would give myself over to slavery in order to tell them as much as I have learned about our Savior. I am ready to do this because I firmly believe that the Word of the Cross is able to rescue souls even in degraded conditions. I also thought that even if I would not be of use to anyone in particular, I could test my obedience to our Savior through this; but my main reason for going would be because there are still souls in the islands that cannot believe because they have not heard.

The leader of the young men's choir did not like the idea of Leonhard leaving Herrnhut. He was a valuable youth, both for his working skills and his godly example among the rest. But after a year of waiting the congregation allowed Leonhard to draw lots concerning his future. The slip of paper he pulled out said: "Let the boy go, the Lord is with him." David Nitschmann was chosen to go with him.

With dread and excitement the two men first saw the palm-fringed shore of St. Thomas on December 13, 1732. Recently purchased from France, together with the islands of St. Croix and St. John, this most prosperous island of the West Indies already supplied all of Denmark with sugar and tobacco. Dutch Reformed families, owners of its one hundred and fifty plantations, lived in airy mansions surrounded by the cane-thatched mud huts of black slaves whom they firmly believed "predestined to perdition." Every month, new shiploads of captives from Africa arrived at St. Thomas's harbor. Those who turned deathly sick en route were tossed overboard to save on food and water. Those who survived were led – skin and bones, eyes glazed with terror – onto the wharves of St. Thomas and placed at the mercy of "Christian" landlords who promptly broke them in to work.

Under the vigilant eye of Jan Borm, Reformed pastor of the island, strict Calvinist rule kept all in their places – slaves subject to masters, and masters subject to God and the church as they understood it. Blacks enjoyed few liberties and no luxuries. Deprived of furniture, bedding, decent clothing, and utensils, slaves were forced to sleep on the ground and eat their meals with their hands. Small pox, lockjaw, and leprosy killed many.

Outnumbered six to one by their black slaves, white slave owners lived in perpetual fear of revolt. St. Thomas law required the cutting off of slaves' hands lifted against their owners. First-time runaways had one foot cut off. Subsequent attempts resulted in cutting off the second foot, then one leg after the other. Floggings occurred every week – five hundred lashes (permitted by law) being equal to a death sentence. After less severe floggings, slave owners were known to rub salt and pepper in the wounds.

St. Thomas law required the prompt execution of slaves planning revolt – their owners to be paid by the government for every slave decapitated or hanged. The same law fined people fifty pounds of tobacco for working on the Lord's Day (Sunday), and obligated all whites to attend church. Order, greed, and terror in the name of God – the two brothers from Herrnhut felt it enveloping them at once and wondered what place they would find in it.

Leonhard and David were not able to sell themselves into slavery because of a Dutch law prohibiting the enslavement of white people, but a Dutch planter hired them to finish a new house he had built and gave them a place to sleep. Then, at the first opportunity, they set out with a letter from Anton to look for his brother and sister. On a plantation on the south side of the island, the young men found them. Not only were they amazed to hear from their brother in Europe; they listened open-mouthed to Leonhard's stories of the Savior. Then they called more of their family and friends together. Even though they could barely understand Leonhard's mixture of German and Dutch (the slaves spoke a Dutch creole), they received Christ's promise of good news for the poor with joy and gave their lives to him.

The awakening among the slaves kept on spreading. It spread much faster than anyone expected, and certainly faster than any white people on the island liked. White Christians who owned the slaves felt convicted. Many of them lived in shameless debauchery. "How can you black devils live up to the gospel," they asked, "when even we white people, to whom it was given, cannot do it?" Other slave owners, proud of their Christianity and of the fair treatment they gave their slaves, felt encroached upon by the missionaries' work. "Our slaves are happy," they insisted. "They have it much better with us than they did in Africa. So why come and stir up discontent?"

Some slave owners flogged their slaves for attending Moravian meetings. Nearly all took their books away if they caught them learning to read – one slave owner making it a practice to set the books on fire and swat them in his slaves' faces. "That," he said, "is how my slaves will learn to read." Converts were deliberately sold to other West Indian islands to separate them from Christian fellowship. And mobs of drunken white men regularly broke up meetings.

Despite all this, the crowds of seekers that gathered in the evenings to learn of Christ grew ever larger. Not only did the congregation include both African and island-born slaves – it included people of many different tribes and customs. The first two baptisms on St. Thomas already brought members of the Mandinga, Mangree, Fante, Atja, Kassenti, Tjamba, Amina, Watje, and Loango tribes into the church.

In 1738, at the suggestion of a former slave and with help from Herrnhut, the Moravians managed to buy several of the baptized slaves and a small cotton plantation on the central and highest part of the island. Such rejoicing broke out among the black believers at the purchase of the land that a meeting for praise lasted until the sun came up the following morning. Now they had a place to gather undisturbed. Hundreds came for every meeting, the sick carried on shoulders and one-legged former runaways hobbling in on canes (one man had lost both feet in punishment and could only crawl). Because they used trumpets to announce meetings there, the believers named their new community on the hill the Posaunenberg (mountain of trumpets). But the days of peace and rejoicing wouldn't last long.

Two Moravian brothers, Friedrich Martin and Matthäus Freundlich, had decided to take in the abandoned children they found starving during the drought of 1737. They hired Rebecca, a mulatto woman who had been freed from slavery at age twelve and joined the Moravians as a teenager, to take care of the children. The following year, she and Matthäus were married. Friedrich, who had been ordained a minister, performed the ceremony, and they began their life together with nine adopted children. Rebecca became a leading evangelist for the Moravian mission and provided pastoral care to women in the church.

Led by their pastor, Jan Borm, the white people of St. Thomas determined to get rid of Moravian influence on their plantations once and for all. The case they picked for their excuse was the marriage of Matthäus and Rebecca Freundlich. "Since when is it lawful for a white man to marry a black woman?" asked angry islanders (many of whom had mulatto children from numerous concubines). "What is more, who authorized Friedrich Martin to marry them?"

Dragged before the St. Thomas court, Friedrich, Matthäus, and Rebecca all refused to swear an oath and soon found themselves in a putrid cell, hot as an oven during the day, with nothing to sleep on at night. Great crowds of slaves risked punishment to come to the barred window of their cell to listen to the prisoners' preaching and words of encouragement. Their example of peaceful non-resistance deeply inspired the believers, now numbering 750 souls on fifty-one plantations, under the able leadership of two black brothers, Christoph and Mingo.

With the German brothers in jail, Jan Borm and the Protestant officials wasted no time in doing what they could to bring the black congregation to ruin. The pastor had black believers brought before the court, one by one. In particular, he interrogated the leaders, throwing complicated theological questions at them to see how they would respond. On top of that he asked them to explain which faith was more biblical, the Lutheran or the Reformed, and whether they thought black people would someday rule whites.

"We know nothing about religion," the black Christians answered him, "except that the Lamb of God has died and taken our sins away. We do not know whether blacks will ever rule whites, but we know that after death we will stand before Christ, where all men are equal."

"See, they know nothing," Pastor Borm rejoiced. "Those Herrn-hut prophets are baptizing untaught savages!"

The court sentenced Matthäus and Rebecca as a public nuisance, living in unlawful immorality, and ordered Matthäus to pay a fine. Rebecca, who had earlier worshiped in the Reformed Church, was formally excommunicated and ordered to be sold as a slave. Friedrich Martin was to be held for punishment and exile, but was later released because his health was so poor.

A few weeks later the trade winds carried an unexpected ship into St. Thomas's harbor. People from Germany – and, it soon became apparent, very important people – stepped onto the wharf. The governor, hiding his displeasure as well as possible, could do nothing but formally welcome Count Nikolaus Ludwig von Zinzendorf to St. Thomas.

The St. Thomas authorities knew that the count came directly from Herrnhut. They also knew he enjoyed the favor of the Danish court and that in rank he stood far above any of them. So when Zinzendorf cheerfully asked for the release of Matthäus and Rebecca, they granted it promptly and said no more about it.

Arriving on the ship with Zinzendorf were Veronika Löhans, her husband Valentin, and another Moravian couple. It would be only a few months before Veronika would experience the assault recounted at the beginning of this story.

By 1768, seventy-nine missionaries sent out from Herrnhut had lost their lives in the West Indies due to hardship and tropical diseases. But for every one that died there were sixty baptized converts. Within fifty years nearly nine thousand African slaves on St. Thomas alone had found their way into the church community.

Written by Peter Hoover

16

Jacob Hochstetler

suffered 1757, in Pennsylvania

IN 1682, AN EARLY QUAKER named William Penn bought a large province in the Americas, making him the world's largest private landowner. He named this tract of land "Sylvania," but King Charles II of England insisted that it be called Pennsylvania in honor of its new owner. To develop this expansive piece of real estate, William Penn traveled Europe, appealing to oppressed minorities with promises of religious freedom and potential wealth in his new holdings. Quakers, Huguenots, Lutherans, and Jews all responded to his invitation, and soon settlers began making the fifty-day ocean voyage across the Atlantic to reach the new colony.

Four decades after Penn's purchase, Jacob Hochstetler, an Amish man living with his young family in Switzerland, responded to William Penn's promise of freedom from religious persecution. The Amish were followers of Jakob Ammann, an Anabaptist leader who called church members to return to the clear convictions that had defined the movement's faith and practices at the time of Menno Simons a century before. The year 1728 had seen the beginning of increased persecution of the Amish in Switzerland, and Jacob Hochstetler believed he could find peace and a more prosperous life for himself, his wife, and their three-year-old son in Pennsylvania.

Jacob's family set out on a ship from Rotterdam with 388 men, women, and children, arriving in Philadelphia on September 1, 1736. Although he and his family took a few years to find their bearings in this new land, Jacob eventually purchased property east of the Northkill River, on the western edge of the area inhabited by Europeans.

Life in the American wilderness was not easy. Jacob built his homestead near a spring and removed much of the surrounding forest. He converted the cleared land into groves of fruit trees. There was no school in the area for the children to attend – Jacob was now a father of three boys and a girl – but he and his wife taught their children a variety of subjects at home, including how to write in German. Despite the hardships of frontier life, they were able to worship God as they desired, free from oppression.

At the time, large portions of Pennsylvania were inhabited by a native tribe called the Delawares, who referred to themselves as *Lenni Lenape,* the "original people." Members of this tribe occasionally visited the Hochstetler homestead. For a while, relations were good between the natives and the new inhabitants of William Penn's province. When white settlers caused any aggravation to the Delaware people or vice versa, each group dealt with their offenders appropriately.

The harmony did not last. To the west, along the Ohio River, a border dispute broke out between the French and the English. The French sought the allegiance of local tribes by offering better terms of trade than the English. The tribes defeated the British army under General Braddock, and so believed they could drive all settlers from their land. They pushed east and began attacking settlements. By 1757 the Northkill settlers had received reports of natives killing, scalping, and kidnapping hundreds of settlers in nearby townships.

Summer brought a temporary lull in the violence, and fall came. On the evening of September 19, 1757, young people from surrounding homesteads had gathered at the Hochstetler home to pare and slice apples from the family orchard for drying. Once the work was done, the visitors socialized until late, then left to return to their own homes. Not long after the family went to bed, their dog started growling. One of the three sons, Jacob Jr., went to investigate. As he opened the front door, a gunshot cracked through the night air. He fell back with a bullet in his leg. Guessing that members of the Delaware tribe, once their friends, were now attacking their home, he barred the door. The rest of the family gathered to investigate. Through a window they counted a dozen or so men huddled in the dark near the outdoor bake oven, in urgent debate.

Two of the sons, Joseph and Christian, reached for their hunting rifles so they could mount a defense. But their father would have none of it. Describing this moment in a 1912 biography, a descendant, Harvey Hostetler, captured Jacob's terrible dilemma:

[Jacob] met a severe temptation on the night his home was attacked by the Indians. His son Jacob had been wounded by the Indians, who sought his life and the life of the entire family. The family was secure in the house and could easily see the Indians standing a short distance away, within easy range and reach of the weapons in the hands of the family. Perhaps a few shots in the air or in the direction of the foe might have driven them away. At any rate the family might easily have put up a hard fight. All the natural instincts impel men to fight and defend themselves and their families when attacked. How came it that this frontiersman, accustomed to firearms and skilled in their use, did not yield to the

> entreaties of his sons that they be allowed to defend the family? ...
> Under these conditions his allegiance to his Lord rose supreme
> and he was enabled to continue his trust in God. To his credit be
> it said, he remained true to what he believed to be right. He would
> not disobey God, who had said, "Thou shalt not kill."

Jacob overcame the temptation to use firearms. He reminded his
sons that they must never kill a human being, even in self-defense.
They begged him, but he was resolute, and they left their weapons
where they were. Looking back on the incident years later, Joseph
was certain that if their father had given his consent for them to
fight, they could have saved the entire family.

The men outside seemed to reach an agreement. Gathering some
kindling, they set the house on fire. The family inside retreated to
the cellar. When the fire came through the floor, they poured cider
on the flames. As the sun crept over the horizon, Jacob saw the
aggressors departing. When the fire could no longer be held back,
he started helping each member of the family through the small
cellar window. The first to emerge made eye contact with the single
remaining attacker, a young Delaware man who had stayed behind
to gather peaches from the surrounding trees.

The man shouted the alarm, and the rest of the family rushed to
escape the smoking cellar. Jacob's wife struggled to fit through the
small opening, and the son whose leg had been injured also needed
assistance. By the time they had all emerged from the cellar, they
were surrounded by the enemy. Joseph, an athletic boy, was the
only one to escape. He outran two pursuers and hid in the woods
behind a log.

Back at the house, the attackers tomahawked and scalped the
Hochstetler's daughter and Jacob, the son who had been shot in the
leg. Then they stabbed the mother with a butcher knife and scalped
her as well.

The attackers took the father Jacob and his son Christian captive.
They surrounded Joseph's hiding spot and took him prisoner too.

Before leaving, the three prisoners grabbed some peaches and stuffed them in their pockets. Then their captors bound their hands and led them into the mountains.

When new captives were brought into Native American villages, it was common for the community to gather. Some prisoners were made to run the gauntlet, passing between two lines of villagers, who beat the new arrivals with sticks and other objects as they passed through. Expecting this reception, Jacob and his sons offered the peaches they'd gathered to the chief and those surrounding him. Honored by the gift, the chief ordered that they not be abused.

Jacob and his sons were then separated, but not before he gave them one last piece of advice: "If you are taken so far away and kept so long that you forget your German language, do not forget the Lord's Prayer." The father and his sons would not see each other again until many years later.

The captives were forced to conform to the tribe's customs and dress. Jacob's captors pulled his beard out – one bit at a time, as if plucking a bird – along with most of the hair on his head, only leaving a patch four inches wide, which was then braided as it grew. The two sons were soon acculturated to indigenous life. Joseph, whose athletic prowess and backwoods skill had helped him elude capture at first, was quickly adopted into the tribe. Christian, about ten years old when he was captured, was adopted by an old Delaware man. The boy hunted to feed the two of them, and the old man embraced him as a son. Both Joseph and Christian grew increasingly fond of the Delaware people during their time with them, and they were treated as members of the tribe.

Jacob, on the other hand, never lost his will to escape. When the men of the tribe went on raiding parties, he was expected to hunt during the days. When he returned at the end of the day, he had to explain how every bullet was used – if any were missing, he needed a good reason. Day after day, he stored a little gunpowder and a bullet or two in a hollowed-out tree, inventing excuses for why they were missing at the end of the day. Finally, he decided he'd stored enough to make his escape.

His captors had never revealed where they were keeping him, so when he struck out on his own, he had to use what little information he'd overheard to gain his bearings. He set off with a fellow prisoner and co-conspirator, John Specht. The first night, they prepared a camp under a secluded rock overhang. But despite their attempts to hide their fire, a lone tribesman wandered upon their camp.

The two escapees did their best to conceal their intentions, and set off in separate directions as if to gather wood for the fire. Speaking in German, they arranged to meet up at a nearby brook. Jacob arrived at their meeting point first. After waiting for his companion for several hours, Jacob came back to the camp they had left. In the dimming light of the fire, he saw blood. Specht had been caught and killed.

He set off alone, walking in the direction he hoped would take him to an English fort or settlement. Going was slow, because he diligently took time to cover his tracks, even after he was far away from the Delaware village. Coming to what he believed was the Ohio, but was in fact the Susquehanna River, he built a makeshift raft and floated downstream on it. He ate whatever he could find, but soon became famished and exhausted from travel. Eventually, he drifted past a fort, but was too weak to stand or make his presence known. Then, farther downriver, his raft passed a man watering his horse. All Jacob could manage was to raise his hand, but it was enough. He was rescued, and eventually returned home.

In 1758, a series of English victories all but ended the conflict now known as the French and Indian War. The settlers of Pennsylvania negotiated for the release of all family members held captive by native tribes, but initially few people were actually returned. In 1762 Jacob petitioned the governor for the release of his two sons, but only Christian was returned. In 1763 Ottawa chief Pontiac initiated a second confrontation, further delaying the return of Joseph. A year later, the area tribes were defeated by Colonel Henry Bouquet, and the Delaware chiefs returned their captives. Joseph Hochstetler was reunited with his father, though his years among the Delaware made it difficult for him to return to the culture of his family.

Today many of Jacob's descendants are found among the Amish, Mennonites, and Brethren of North America, carrying on his resolute commitment to living faithfully and peaceably, whatever the cost.

17

Gnadenhütten

1782, in Ohio

ON MARCH 8, 1782, less than six years after the founding of the United States of America, ninety-six Native American Christians who had embraced Jesus' way of nonresistance were slaughtered by settlers in Ohio, in reprisal for an attack carried out by a different group of Native Americans.

Sadly, the massacre also effectively ended a fifty-year effort by the Moravian church to bring Europeans and Native Americans together as brothers and sisters in Christian community. News of the event spread from tribe to tribe, and Native Americans no longer trusted the promises of white people. Two decades later the Shawnee chief Tecumseh reminded William Henry Harrison (the future president): "You recall the time when the Jesus Indians of the Delawares lived near the Americans, and had confidence in their promises of friendship, and thought they were secure, yet the

99

Americans murdered all the men, women, and children, even as they prayed to Jesus?"

Today little trace remains of the Moravians' exceptional witness to brotherhood between immigrants and the First Peoples of North America other than monuments. The most important of these historical markers were erected to honor the martyrs of two different places named Gnadenhütten (houses of grace). In Pennsylvania, white Moravians were killed by Native Americans. In Ohio, their Native American brethren were killed by white Americans. In both cases, the martyrs were men, women, and children who tried to follow the way of Christ in a violent and dangerous time, looking past differences in skin color, language, and customs to call one another brothers and sisters. They were prepared to sacrifice their own lives rather than take the lives of others.

The Native Americans killed in Ohio, who had fled west to escape violence, had named their new settlement after the martyrs of Gnadenhütten, Pennsylvania, where twenty-six years earlier, on November 24, 1755, ten Moravian missionaries and a child were murdered and their homes burned to the ground.

One of the survivors of that attack, Susanne Partsch, had left her home in Germany ten years earlier to join the mission to the New World, and had recently agreed to serve as cook for the missionaries in Gnadenhütten on Mahoning Creek (near modern-day Lehighton). She and her husband, George, had been at Gnadenhütten less than a week when a Native American war party attacked the settlement. Susanne saw the men "running from one house to another with firebrands to set them alight." The church, school, bakery, and dwellings were reduced to ashes. Cattle were slaughtered, and food, tools, and supplies were taken or ruined. Some of the residents, including an infant, were burned alive in their homes. The Moravians had some warning of the impending violence, but had decided not to abandon their mission.

Susanne saved herself by leaping from a second-story window and hiding in a hollow tree until the next morning, when a local militiaman found her and took her back to the settlement. She wrote of her experience, "I fainted at the sight of the charred bodies, and they had trouble bringing me back to my senses." She found that her husband had also survived, but another member of the church, Susanna Nitschmann, had been taken into captivity as a prize of war. She was abused so severely by her captor that she never fully recovered. Her husband was among those murdered.

The massacre on the Mahoning was a minor event in a much larger conflict between France and England called the Seven Years War, known in America as the French and Indian War. American colonists fought alongside British troops and Native American allies against the French and their Native American allies. Each native tribe faced a decision whether to fight for the British, who claimed to rule North America, or to resist them. They were victims of this war between European empires that set tribe against tribe.

For some Native Americans, most notably Chief Teedyuscung, this was an opportunity to reclaim ancestral lands that had been stolen. Before the war Teedyuscung had converted to Christianity and for a time lived with the Moravians at Gnadenhütten, but he objected to their teaching on nonviolence, which he felt was undermining the resolve and courage of his people, the Lenape (or Delaware). When the Delaware were attacked by other tribes, the Moravians urged them not to resist, which offended Teedyuscung. He rejected Moravian nonresistance and began raiding white and indigenous settlements.

The assault on Gnadenhütten was one of several Native American attacks on European settlers on the Pennsylvania frontier, but it is noteworthy because of the unusual response to the massacre. The Moravians at Bethlehem, the group's headquarters in North America and a thriving intentional community, were horrified by the news of what had happened to their brothers and sisters at

Gnadenhütten, about twenty-five miles away. Soon Native American and white refugees began arriving at Bethlehem, seeking food, shelter, and protection. George and Susanne Partsch were among them. Susanne "felt wretched and had to bear a serious illness." Rather than being defeated by their ordeal, however, the Partsches set out again as missionaries just a few years later, this time to slaves in the Virgin Islands.

Eventually seventy indigenous converts from the Gnadenhütten area made their way to Bethlehem, seeking protection from white reprisals for the massacre. The presence of these Native American refugees must have sorely tested the goodwill of some of the Bethlehem people: not only had their brothers and sisters just been massacred by members of this tribe, but they lived under constant fear of a similar attack on their own settlement. Bishop August Gottlieb Spangenberg urged his brethren not to close their hearts to these refugees, who had been driven from their homes by the war. The Moravians, sometimes reluctantly, continued to love the refugees as they knew Christ did. They protected the Native Americans from whites who were intent on revenge, but they also welcomed non-Moravian colonists who were fleeing the violence on the frontier. In all, about eight hundred people, both natives and colonists, were sheltered in the communities of Bethlehem and nearby Nazareth. This was a rare instance of Europeans and Native Americans seeking refuge together from the violence of the age.

The Moravians relieved some of the overcrowding in the Bethlehem commune by helping the Native Americans build a village called Nain one mile from town. There they could live according to their culture and traditions while still worshiping as Moravians. It took a while to find a suitable spot and clear the land for building, but finally, in October 1758, the chapel was dedicated in Nain.

Nearby settlers objected to Nain, and so did some native leaders. Teedyuscung tried in vain to persuade his people to leave the village. Then, in 1763, the governor of Pennsylvania insisted that the Moravians bring their Native American members to Philadelphia to protect them from the ravages of the Paxton Boys, a white vigilante group that was intent on slaughtering natives. Conditions in the refugee camp in Philadelphia were grim, however, and eventually Moravian missionary David Zeisberger was allowed to take his flock of sick and harassed people out of Pennsylvania. They settled in Ohio in the early 1770s.

Who were these Moravians who found themselves in the midst of controversy and violence on the American frontier? In 1722 a group of Protestants tracing their roots to Jan Hus fled persecution in Moravia and were granted refuge on the estate of Count Nikolaus von Zinzendorf in Germany. There they built a village called Herrnhut, which became a unique form of Christian community. Everyone who agreed to live according to the Brotherly Agreement, ratified in 1727, was welcomed regardless of their church affiliation or nationality. The Brotherly Agreement stipulated that the only reason to live in Herrnhut was service to Christ.

That same year the Herrnhut residents experienced a spiritual renewal that inspired them to embark on an extraordinary fifty-year period of global mission. In 1740 the first Moravians arrived in Pennsylvania, and the next year they began the community of Bethlehem, which was to be the base for an extensive mission network. Dozens of Moravians learned Native American languages and some were adopted into various tribes in the Iroquois Confederacy.

Bethlehem was not only the economic and administrative headquarters for the Moravian mission in North America; it was intended to be a "city on the hill." It was a very effective Christian commune for about twenty years. The missionaries built some of the largest buildings in colonial Pennsylvania to house the hundreds of men, women, and children who lived together under the Brotherly Agreement. Some of the residents agreed to stay there permanently to raise crops and provide support for the church, while others were "pilgrims" who agreed to go wherever they were sent. Many of these pilgrims worked with Native Americans, especially among the Lenape people. Bethlehem had a smoothly functioning economy, but no police force, stocks, or jail. Some colonists accused the Moravians of plotting with Native Americans and even arming them, but in reality the truth is the Moravians were people of peace. They refused to join militias or serve in the army, though the church's rules did allow for self-defense and defense of women and children.

The economy and social structure of Bethlehem were severely strained by the influx of refugees, but the community survived. On several occasions Bethlehem was threatened by Native American war parties and white mobs. In order to protect the town from the type of assault suffered at Gnadenhütten, the Moravians built a stockade around the perimeter. Residents kept watch day and night, with orders to fire warning shots if anyone was seen moving against the town.

On Christmas Day in 1755, just weeks after the Gnadenhütten attack, the Moravians in Bethlehem celebrated the birth of Christ in their usual way with the playing of trombones just before dawn. According to later reports, the noise of the brass instruments, often associated with armies, so alarmed a group of people planning a dawn assault that they broke off their planned attack and returned to the woods. This story of trombones thwarting an attack may be more legendary than historical, but it is true that the Moravians continued to worship Christ in the midst of conflict.

In 1776 war again engulfed the British colonies in America, but this time the colonists were fighting against the British army. Once again Native Americans were swept up in a conflict between Europeans. In 1749 the British Parliament had granted Moravians an exemption from military service in recognition of their long-established objection to killing people. During the American

Revolution, they insisted on their right not to fight. On several occasions, though, they were threatened with forced conscription by either the American or British armies and had to pay large indemnities to avoid it. Some were jailed; others fled. One of the buildings in Bethlehem became a hospital for wounded soldiers in both armies, and the Moravians helped bury the war dead from both sides. Apart from that, it appeared that they would be able to avoid being drawn into the maelstrom of revolution and war.

David Zeisberger and his wife Suzanna had led their congregation of Lenape and Mohicans out of Pennsylvania and established a new village on the Tuscarawas River in Ohio in 1772. A Mohican named Joshua led the new community, which was named Gnadenhütten in honor of the martyrs of 1755. The village had grown to over two hundred people, all Native American, by the time war broke out. In 1781, as the war between the British and Americans moved westward, the British forcibly relocated the Gnadenhütten Moravians one hundred miles northwest to Sandusky. Many starved, died of disease, or froze to death during the winter. In the spring over a hundred of the survivors were allowed to return to their village on the Tuscarawas River in the hopes of planting crops and hunting game.

But the specter of war and hatred stalked the land. Several white families were massacred by Native American war parties allied with the British, and an American militia of about 160 people, led by a certain David Williamson, set out to seek revenge. Rather than targeting those who had committed the murders, they decided to attack the peace-loving people of Gnadenhütten. They occupied Gnadenhütten and rounded up other Native Americans from surrounding villages and the woods. On March 7 they held a mock tribunal, convicted the Native American Moravians of murder, and sentenced them to death. The only mercy they showed was that they honored the Christians' request for time to prepare themselves for martyrdom. Throughout the night, the Moravians confessed their sins, comforted one another, and sang hymns to Christ their Savior.

The next day the white militia murdered ninety-six people. Two boys managed to hide under bodies and pretended to be dead. They bore witness to the atrocity and to the courage of the martyrs. There were two "killing houses," one for men and one for women. Most were killed by mallets or tomahawks. The executioners also scalped their victims in order to take prizes home. Some of those scalped were still alive. Nearly half of the victims were children. According to one participant, "Nathan Rollins had tomahawked nineteen of the poor Moravians, and after it was over he sat down and cried, and said it was no satisfaction for the loss of his father and uncle after all." When the killing spree was over, the militia looted the town and burned the buildings with the bodies in them.

After the war, Moravian missionary John Heckewelder returned to the site and buried the remains of the martyrs. None of the white people who participated in the massacre were brought to justice, but some were killed in revenge by non-Moravian Lenape. The British authorities granted Zeisberger, who had not been present at the time of the massacre, permission to take the remnant of his Lenape and Mohican congregation to Canada, where they would be safer.

The martyrs of two different places named Gnadenhütten were prepared to sacrifice their own lives rather than take the lives of others. They knew there are things worth dying for but not worth killing for. Although their deaths remain a shameful chapter of American history, we can view them as victors rather than victims, for they joined the ranks of thousands of Christian martyrs who witnessed in life and death to their faith in Christ by loving their enemies and praying for those who persecuted them.

Written by Craig Atwood

18

Joseph and Michael Hofer

died 1918, in Kansas, United States

JACOB WIPF AND THREE BROTHERS, David, Joseph, and Michael Hofer, all members of the Hutterite Rockport Colony in South Dakota, were called to war on May 25, 1918.

All the men were thirty or younger, with wives and children at home. But when asked by the draft board whether they were the sole providers for their families, each of the men answered "no," since they knew that their church would step in to help if they were gone. With this response, the chance of a near-certain exemption passed them by.

The four men traveled along dirt roads fom their communal home to the nearby town of Alexandria, where scores of their neighbors gathered for a patriotic rally to cheer on local men heading off to war. The four Hutterites from Rockport Colony and their friend Andrew Wurtz, whom they met at the station, looked different from the other young men. They were dressed in black and wore beards, symbols of their commitment to living out the peaceable kingdom of God. The Hutterites had been directed by their ministers and family members to report to the camp as required, but to do nothing to advance the war effort. To do so would be to disobey Christ's commands to love the enemy and reject violence.

Such convictions earned more hostility than admiration amid the nation's wartime patriotism. Only weeks before, the Liberty Loan Committee of nearby Hanson County had illegally confiscated a hundred steers and a thousand sheep from a Hutterite settlement whose members refused to buy war bonds. And on May 25, 1918, the very day that the men left South Dakota for Camp Lewis in Washington State, the South Dakota Council of Defense banned the use of German, "the enemy language," in the state. The Hutterites, who worshiped and taught in German, were a clear target of the legislation.

Knowing all this, the Hofer brothers and Jacob Wipf had reason to be wary as they climbed on the train for Camp Lewis. In their own minds, their arrival at the camp would be the moment when they would testify to their faith and their refusal to serve as soldiers. To the American government, however, they had ceased to be civilians from the moment they received their conscription papers. As the fifteen-car train started heading west, the four men were moved from one Pullman coach to the next. The recruits in each car heckled the Hutterites, well known in this part of the country as pacifists and German speakers. The conductor finally found a small compartment where the men could be by themselves.

Later that day, though, a band of fellow recruits wished to speak with the Hutterites, who knew two of the men, William Danforth and James Albert Montgomery, from their hometown. The Hutterites at first declined to open the door. When they finally did, the new recruits stormed in, speaking of a "free barbering." They forcibly removed the Hutterites from the car, shaving their beards and cutting their hair.

The train continued on, reaching Washington. Recruits from across the West were pouring into Camp Lewis, an impressive seventy-thousand-acre training camp. On May 28, the Hofer brothers and Jacob Wipf entered this khaki city where tens of thousands of young men were being trained, many of them as infantrymen bound for Europe.

When they arrived, the recruits were told to line up alphabetically in preparation for filling out enlistment and assignment cards. The Hutterites stepped away from the line, sensing that to do otherwise would be to line up as soldiers in the US Army. They refused to fill out the cards, which were titled "Statement of Soldier." Officers tried to persuade the men to follow orders, but to no avail. President Woodrow Wilson and Newton Baker, the Secretary of War, expected each man to do his part in the war effort, including conscientious objectors, who might be assigned to kitchen duty or maintenance. The camp commanders seem to have been exasperated by the Hutterites' blanket refusal to participate in camp life. The commanders said they had no choice but to lock up the men because of their refusal to obey orders. So while Camp Lewis prepared for war, the Hutterites remained in the guardhouse, awaiting trial.

From the guardhouse, David Hofer wrote to his wife, Anna:

> If you think about where we are, far from home and farm, from wife and children, then I can't describe the misery in which we find ourselves. We have already been seriously challenged by various things, but with God's help are remaining faithful to him and our vow not to abandon our promise, let it cost body and life. . . . For our dear Savior says, in Matthew 5, "Blessed are those who are persecuted for righteousness' sake, for the kingdom of God is theirs." I must close now with my simple writing and one has to be careful what we write, and we can't write very often, not as often as we would hope. We are being court-martialed, for five to twenty-five years in jail.

The authorities charged the Hutterites with disobeying orders and thus violating the Articles of War. In the court-martial trial, officers recounted their efforts to persuade the men to line up and fill out the requisite forms. Jacob Wipf was the first defendant to take the stand. An untraveled farmer whose mother tongue was German and who had only a grade-school education, he now had to face a panel of officers. The prosecutor wanted to know exactly why the men would not serve in the armed forces in any capacity.

"Are you willing to take part in any noncombatant branch of the service of the army?"

"No; we can't."

"What are your reasons?"

"Well, it is all for war. The only thing we can do is work on a farm for the poor and needy ones of the United States."

"What do you mean by poor and needy ones?"

"Well, those that can't help themselves."

"Would you include soldiers who are crippled for life?"

"Yes. They are poor and needy ones. . . ."

"If you were in the service, such as the Medical Corps, where you would attend the wounded soldiers, would your conscience and the teachings of the church permit that?"

"We can't do that, because a soldier, he will go and fight, and that is helping the war, and we can't do that."

"And if there were wounded soldiers about, you couldn't help them? You couldn't help them because you would be afraid they might recover and go back to the war; is that it?"

"Well, it would be helping the war."

"Would you be willing to be placed on a farm by the government and grow wheat for soldiers?"

"No."

"Does your religion believe in fighting of any kind?"

"No."

"You would not fight with your fists?"

"Well, we ain't no angels. Little boys will scrap sometimes, and we are punished; but our religion don't allow it."

"If a man was attacking or assaulting your sister, would you fight?"

"No."

"Would you kill him?"

"No."

"What would you do?"

"Well, in a way, if I could get her away, I might hold him. If I was man enough, I would do that. If I couldn't, I would have to let go. We can't kill. That is strictly against our religion."

The four men were found guilty of all charges. Their sentence was dishonorable discharge, loss of all pay, and prison. Michael Hofer shared the news with Maria:

> On Saturday they came and announced to us our punishment, namely, twenty years of hard labor in the prison at Alcatraz, California. God the heavenly Father knows what still awaits us. But we must put our trust in him and accept with patience whatever he allows to happen to us. We are completely yielded to the Lord. Whatever burdens he gives, he also provides a way out so that we can endure it. . . . We only make our cross and suffering more difficult if we are sad. For God will also be with us there (that is, in Alcatraz). He has promised to his own, that when they pass through the fire, he will stand beside them so that the flames do not burn them.

Meanwhile, Andrew Wurtz, who had been separated from the Hofer brothers and Jacob Wipf after their arrival at Camp Lewis, faced his own trial. He described extreme physical measures applied to persuade him to work: being forcibly dunked in cold water, being pulled across floor boards to drive splinters into his skin, and more. Eventually he agreed to work in the camp garden, but only alone, not in the company of men in uniform.

After two months at Camp Lewis, the four men left for Alcatraz. They were chained together in pairs and traveled in the escort of four armed lieutenants, arriving two days later at the notorious island in San Francisco Bay. Alcatraz was one of three detention centers for military prisoners, known for its progressive management. Under its commandant, Colonel Garrard, inmates – referred to as "disciples" – enjoyed access to vocational training programs, classical concerts, and a large library. However, these benefits did not extend to the four conscientious objectors.

On arrival, the four men climbed a series of switchbacks to reach the prison building on top of the island. Once inside they were unwilling to put on uniforms or to work. Guards took them along a corridor of stacked cells to a staircase that led to the basement of the prison, the dungeon, a place of solitary confinement known as "the hole." Each man entered a cell under a sloping brick arch, six feet high at the uppermost point. The cells themselves measured six and a half feet wide by eight feet deep. They were cold and wet, but the men declined to put on the uniforms that lay on the floor beside them. In the early days, the men received half a glass of water each day but no food.

The men were chained to the bars, one hand crossed over the other. The chains were drawn up so that only their toes touched the floor, a technique called "high cuffing," long familiar in the history of torture. David Hofer tried to move the toilet pail closer so that he could stand on it to relieve the pain in his arms. Living in darkness by day and by night, the men received periodic visits from guards, who reportedly came at least once with knotted lashes, striking the men. When the guards led the men outside after their first five days in solitary confinement, the prisoners' arms were too swollen to fit in their jackets.

From Alcatraz, Joseph Hofer shared only a sense of general hardship in writing to his wife, Maria. Like his brothers, Joseph omitted details of their solitary imprisonment; or it may be that prison officials excised any unpleasant or incriminating details from the outgoing letters. He wrote:

> My precious and dear wife, I am still in prison and I do not know if we will ever see each other again. Let us hope that we will; but if not in this world, then in that yonder place where no one will separate us from each other. But in order to get there we must put off all desires of the flesh, and take the cross upon ourselves, along with the hatred and taunting of the world, and look up to Jesus our Savior and to his apostles, and to our forefathers, as Paul says in Hebrews 12. For we have a cloud of witnesses before us. And you will find there that all those who found pleasure with God had to suffer affliction. Now, my best wishes to you and to all those who read this letter. Amen.

The Hofer brothers (or, as they were known in Alcatraz, Nos. 15238, 15239, and 15240) and Jacob Wipf (No. 15237) provided scarcely a glimpse at this time of their traumatic life at Alcatraz. There is no mention in their letters of what would later come to light: sleeping on wet concrete in their underwear, standing for hours in chains, being beaten by guards.

On Armistice Day, November 11, 1918, residents of San Francisco gathered to celebrate the end of the war with rounds of "Auld Lang Syne." Three days after the armistice, the Hutterites were transferred to Fort Leavenworth in Kansas, still in chains. During the train ride, Michael Hofer wrote his final letter:

> Grace and peace be with you. I want to write to you that we are now on the way to Fort Leavenworth. We don't know, however, what will become of us there. Only God the Almighty knows if we will see each other again in this world, for we go from one affliction to the other. We plead earnestly to God, for he has promised us that not a single hair falls from our heads without his will. And if we do not see each other again in this world, then we will see one another in the next world.

Joseph, likewise, wrote his final letter home, to Maria:

> And when you look at our scrawling you can well imagine how low
> our spirits are, for we are where the waves are roaring and in that
> time when the seas throw up the dead – if you can only see this
> in the right way. This is all for this time, my dear wife. . . My best
> greetings to you and our dear children, father and mother and all
> the brothers and sisters in the faith.

The men arrived at Fort Leavenworth around midnight on
November 19. Though the accounts of what happened next differ,
David Hofer described a march through the streets to the barracks
and then a long wait outdoors before prison clothing arrived.
Michael and Joseph Hofer complained of sharp pain in their chests
soon after their arrival. They were transferred to the hospital.
David Hofer and Jacob Wipf were placed again in solitary confine-
ment when they said they could do no work at the fort.

Michael's and Joseph's condition deteriorated. David sent a
telegram urging family members to come quickly. They arrived
on November 28. Joseph was barely able to communicate. Michael
was not much better. The following morning, when Joseph's wife,
Maria, went to see him, he was dead. At first prison officials did not
want to let her see his body. She persisted and found, to her dismay,
in approaching the coffin, that in death he had been dressed in a
military uniform. A few days later, on December 2, Michael died.

The Office of the Surgeon of the Disciplinary Barracks listed
pneumonia as the cause of death for both men, a common designa-
tion for the Spanish influenza then sweeping through the prison.
The Hutterite church, however, was convinced that the men died
because of mistreatment by the United States military in the
months leading up to their deaths. David was released to accompany the bodies of his brothers back to South Dakota.

Joseph and Michael Hofer

No representative of the United States government ever apologized to the Hofer brothers' families, who would later emigrate to Canada. Fellow church members were quick to absolve President Wilson and Secretary of War Newton Baker of direct responsibility, blaming overzealous generals at the camps. Other observers were less forgiving. Frank Harris, the cosmopolitan editor of the *Saturday Review,* would write in his memoir:

> Is there any doubt as to who is the better man, the brothers Hofer who went through martyrdom to death for their noble belief, or Secretary Baker, who was responsible for their murder? After the facts had been brought before the Secretary [of War] again and again, month after month, day after day, at long last, on December 6, 1918, nearly a month after the war was ended, Secretary Baker found time to issue an order prohibiting cruel corporal punishment, and the handcuffing of prisoners to the bars of their dungeons, etc. Secretary Baker already knew such torture was being practiced, and that it was illegal.

Baker himself expressed few regrets: "I knew the horror of [war] . . . and I have no sympathy whatever, intellectually or sentimentally, with conscientious or any other kind of objection of people who stayed on this side and preferred a place of safety and profit to places of peril and obligation."

When Jacob Wipf was finally released from his "place of safety and profit" in April of 1919, he saw his comrades' graves for himself. Granted clemency by the Office of the Judge Advocate General of the Army, he came home eleven months after his arrest, just in time for spring planting.

Written by Duane Stoltzfus

19

Emanuel Swartzendruber

persecuted 1918, in the United States

ON MARCH 4, 1918 Emanuel Swartzendruber pulled a draft
summons from his mailbox. The letter ordered him to report to
Bad Axe, Michigan. From there he would leave for Camp Greenleaf
in Fort Oglethorpe, Georgia. Although Emanuel was a Mennonite
and abhorred violence of any kind, he honored the summons and
reported to his assigned location as ordered. He and seventeen
other young men traveled by train to Camp Greenleaf.

For his first day in the armed services, Emanuel cleaned toilets
and repaired the sewer system as a member of the sanitation police.
It was hard work, but not unusual for new recruits. That night he
knelt at the foot of his bunk to pray. Other soldiers, hoping to exas-
perate the devout young man, swore at him to drown out his words.

In the morning, the new recruits were led on a tour of noteworthy
Civil War sites. The commanding officer encouraged Emanuel and

his fellow recruits to follow in the footsteps of those past American soldiers. Later, they received another lecture, this time from the military chaplain. He compared the Kaiser to Goliath, the United States to David, and the American soldiers to David's stones he would use to fell the giant. He explained that they were fighting the Lord's battle. To wrap up, he prayed that each of these new recruits would carry home many German skins once the war was over.

It was too much for Emanuel's conscience. The young man knew he could no longer participate in such a glorification of violence. He presented his papers for conscientious objection to his commanding officer, who took him off drill duty and ordered him to work in the kitchen. Emanuel appreciated the respectful gesture, but explained that by preparing meals for soldiers, he was still contributing to military aggression. The officer once again agreed to accommodate Emanuel's conscience. "Watch your bunk so it doesn't run away," were his new orders to the recruit, essentially confining him to quarters. Emanuel's days were long and dull, but despite the occasional jeers of the soldiers, he was content.

A few weeks later, he was transferred to the Medical Officers Training Corps. He discovered that his bunkmate was from the Church of the Brethren, and the two men quickly bonded over their shared faith. They prayed together when they could and encouraged each other in their struggles.

Emanuel's new commanding officer had a reputation for beating "common sense" into conscientious objectors. The sergeant ordered Emanuel and another young man to put on their military uniforms. They refused. This resulted in a severe beating, but Emanuel, seeing that the other young man was not giving in, was encouraged to stand his ground.

After breakfast, Emanuel and three other conscientious objectors were commanded to tear down an outhouse. As they worked, soldiers hit them with pieces of wood. Someone grabbed Emanuel by his trousers and struck his head against the outhouse roof. When the last plank of the toilet was removed, the sergeant said, "Now we'll show you what your Jesus can do when you are in our hands."

He pushed one of the other men into the cesspool. The man sank to his armpits in filth. Other soldiers shoveled excrement onto his head in a mock baptism. One of the onlookers looked upward and jeered, "Can you see Jesus?"

The sergeant commanded the other conscientious objectors to pull the young man out of the filth and take him to the bathhouse. The sergeant followed, throwing soap at Emanuel as he helped clean the abused man. The sargeant forced Emanuel into a corner and choked him with a bar of soap, then dragged him back out to the cesspool. He asked Emanuel if he was now willing to accept military service. The Mennonite was clear. "No."

The sergeant grabbed Emanuel by his ankles and dunked his head into the cesspool. As he lowered Emanuel into the excrement, onlookers shouted, "Don't put him in any further, you'll kill him!" Finally, he pulled Emanuel back up, shaking his head as the poor man coughed and retched. "Go and wash," the sergeant growled.

Later that day, when Emanuel was resting on his bunk, the sergeant passed by and taunted him. "Do you still love me?" Emanuel answered sincerely: "Yes, I do." The sergeant walked away.

When the conscientious objectors were led before a panel of higher officers, they asked the young men what denomination they belonged to. Clearly unsatisfied with their answers, one of the officers turned to the sergeant and ordered: "Put these men on bread and water."

The officers threw Emanuel into the guardhouse, but when that, too, had no effect, he was court-martialed. A military tribunal sentenced him and eight others to ten years of hard labor in Fort Leavenworth, Kansas, forfeiting all payments and allowances.

On their way to Fort Leavenworth, the objectors were held at a jail in Memphis for a few hours. The jailer asked the men what they had done to deserve this treatment. When the prisoners explained their situation, the jailer said, "That's strange. We put people in jail because they fight and you are here because you think it is wrong to fight. If we all believed as you do, we wouldn't need this jail at all."

Later, on the train to Kansas, Emanuel spoke once more with the sergeant who had abused him earlier. The officer said, "When you were first put in the guardhouse, I thought you were nothing but war dodgers. Since then, watching you day by day, I have changed my mind. I used to be a Sunday school boy, but could it be possible that you are right and all the rest of us are wrong about war? I hope they treat you well at Fort Leavenworth."

The sergeant's wish for Emanuel was not to come true. When they reached their destination, the prisoners were put in a big grain bin with several other men and sealed off from the light. They were only given rations of bread and water. Weeks later, Emanuel was assigned to farm labor with a work gang. All day he picked corn and acorns and filled silos with grain.

Two months after his arrival at Fort Leavenworth, the armistice was signed, ending the war in Europe. But Emanuel's ordeal was not over yet. Although he didn't have to serve out the rest of his ten-year sentence, he was sent to Camp Dodge, Iowa, where vindictive officers knew they could treat him poorly until the War Department officially ordered all conscientious objectors released.

Eventually, eleven months after he was first drafted into the United States military, Emanuel Swartzendruber was allowed to return to his home.

20

Regina Rosenberg

died 1919, in Dubovka, Russia

IN MARCH OF 1881, Tsar Alexander II of Russia was traveling through St. Petersburg in his carriage, guarded by armed Cossacks. As his entourage prepared to turn a street corner, an assassin's bomb exploded. Unharmed, the tsar jumped from the carriage to check on the men who had been wounded. In the chaos, someone asked Tsar Alexander if he was injured, and he replied, "Thank God I am untouched." The assassin, Ignacy Hryniewiecki, a member of the Narodnaya Volya (people's will) revolutionary movement, seeing that the tsar was exposed, yelled, "It is too soon to thank God," and hurled a second bomb. The tsar was killed by the blast.

The bomber died from wounds received in the explosion, and many of his revolutionary comrades were imprisoned soon after. But in the eyes of the people, full responsibility for the assassination didn't stop there. Many Russians, already prone to anti-Semitism, blamed the country's Jewish population for the death of the tsar. Their unfounded anger was fueled by the institutional church: the chief procurator of the Russian Orthodox Church cooperated with the police to persecute and preach against Russian Jews.

A bloodbath ensued. Throughout southern Russia, Jewish men, women, and children were shot by the thousands. In Moscow alone, twenty thousand were driven from their homes. Orthodox priests defamed the Jewish people, spreading old rumors: the Jews killed babies, drank blood, and offered Christians as sacrifices. In 1905 the Russian government published a paper called *The Protocols of the Elders of Zion,* supposedly a Jewish plan to overthrow all the world's governments. This document was actually forged, but it was convincing enough to further escalate the terrible pogroms and legalized persecution already in force against Jews in Russia.

Regina Rosenberg, an Orthodox Jew, grew up in this violent and fearful setting. Understandably, she hated Christians as brutal persecutors of her people. However, her parents wanted her to receive a good education, so when an opportunity arose they reluctantly enrolled her in their best option: a local college run by Christians.

Regina was on guard; she assumed that the Christian Bible was filled with blasphemy and slander against Jews. So when a Christian classmate gave her a New Testament, Regina expected to find dreadful lies inside. Instead, as she read she began to realize that Jesus, Paul, and other New Testament writers were themselves Jews. The stories and letters of the Christian Bible actually honored Moses and his law.

Regina's Christian friend convinced her that the Orthodox priests who preached hate-filled sermons against the Jews were not modeling true Christianity. As Regina studied the New Testament in light of the Jewish scriptures and listened to her friend's descriptions of true Christianity, she found herself praying, repenting, and longing to follow Jesus. She became a Christian.

Her family was horrified at her conversion. They did everything they could to pull Regina back into the Jewish fold. Finally, when they realized that there was nothing they could do to turn her from her new faith, they cursed her and cast her out of their home. She took to the streets.

Regina found shelter under bridges and in the ruins of bombed-out buildings. The Great War, later known as the First World War, raged all around her. In Eastern Europe the conflict was nearing its end, but Austria-Hungary had invaded Russia, and civil war had broken out as well: the Red Army of the Bolsheviks had wrested St. Petersburg from the tsar and his White Army.

As Regina traveled among the droves of people displaced by these conflicts, she encountered Jakob and Tina Dyck on the streets of Kharkov. Jakob was Crimean and had been raised among Mennonites. He was a conscientious objector who had consented to serve as a noncombatant in an army hospital. His experiences there had cemented a desire in his heart to work for peace, and now he and his wife, Tina, were traveling through Russia sharing about Christ with other refugees. Regina admired the couple. She decided to join their work.

She journeyed with their group through a world upended by war. Wherever they stopped – camps, towns, and military bases – they held evangelistic meetings. Regina befriended Tina Dyck and Luise Hübert Sukkau, a young woman from a Molochna River Mennonite colony. The size of the group waxed and waned, and they often didn't have food, but they were committed to their mission, working and teaching with enthusiasm. The Mennonites visited hospitals, comforted Russian women whose lives had been destroyed, and preached wherever they could find listeners.

But in the postwar chaos, marauding bands of anarchists were taking advantage of the war-torn villages, burning, looting, and killing. Travel was extremely dangerous. In the fall of 1919, Jakob

Dyck gave the group a choice: they could travel straight on to Luise's Mennonite colony near the Molochna River, where they would find safety and refuge for the winter, or they could prolong their journey, stopping at each of the villages along the way to share the good news of Christ. The second option would drastically increase their chances of encountering a band of raiders. The decision was unanimous – they would stop at the villages.

The group separated into smaller units to more efficiently visit the nearby towns. Regina, Jakob, three brothers, and Luise went to Dubovka, a town with only a few new Christians. Mrs. Peters, a widow, hosted the small band of Mennonites the first night. In the morning, she made breakfast. But before they could eat a bite, a group of anarchists entered the house. They silently sat down around the table with the Christians.

Jakob broke the silence. "We will serve you breakfast," he said, "but we are believers. Before we eat we read from the Bible and pray." The anarchists, loaded with sabers and ammunition belts, didn't say a word, but listened as Jakob read a passage from scripture. When the time came to pray, Regina and her friends stood up. The anarchists did as well, displaying surprising courtesy.

When they had eaten, the uninvited guests demanded that Regina and her friend Luise dance for them. Instead, the two sang. During this serenade, the room filled with more and more armed men. They finished, and Jakob gave a long sermon about Christ's peace. When his voice grew hoarse from speaking, Mrs. Peters brought him two raw eggs to swallow to soothe his throat. The anarchists were fascinated. Some of the men seemed moved by Jakob's words. Eventually, at noon, they left Mrs. Peters's house.

Undeterred by the anarchists' presence in the village – and perhaps even encouraged by their response to Jakob's teaching – Regina and Louise went to the local school to teach a group of children. Jakob soon followed with another missionary. The teacher and his wife welcomed them into the classroom, and they all knelt to pray.

In the meantime, a second group of anarchists burst into Mrs. Peters's home. They beat one of the remaining Christians to the floor, then ordered Mrs. Peters to bandage his wounds with a torn sheet. They forced the beaten man to clean his blood from the floor, then made him lead them to his companions in the school.

"Who gave you permission to hold a meeting here?" asked the anarchist leader as they came into the classroom. They lined Regina, Luise, and the men against a wall. Horrified by what was about to happen, the class's teacher begged the anarchists to spare the children the sight of a bloody execution. The anarchists agreed and took their captives to a barn across the street.

The teacher's wife rushed to a window in another classroom. She watched as Jakob, Regina, and the others complied without resisting. Two anarchists beat Jakob with the butts of their rifles while he covered his face with his hands. Then the group disappeared into the barn. Several shots rang out.

There was a long silence. Then Regina appeared in the barn doorway. One of the anarchists followed, forcing her outside. Through the window, the teacher's wife saw Regina's mouth moving, but she couldn't hear what the young woman was saying to her captor. Again and again, Regina pointed to heaven. The anarchist led her back into the barn.

Two days later, Danilo Astachov and Andrey Epp, two of Jakob Dyck's followers, entered Dubovka. They found a massacre. The houses they entered were filled with dead bodies – eighty-two men, women, and children in total, clumped in small groups. Eventually, the pair entered the barn across from the school.

Inside the door, they found the stripped and mutilated bodies of Jakob Dyck and another man. Further in, they discovered the bodies of another of their friends and Luise Sukkau. Not far from the others, they found the body of Regina Rosenberg. Her neck was slashed, and her head was split with a gaping wound. But her body was not crumpled on the ground like the others. It still rested on its knees in a posture of prayer.

21

Eberhard and Emmy Arnold

persecuted during the 1930s, in Germany

EBERHARD ARNOLD was born in 1883 in Königsberg, East Prussia, into an academic family. To his parents' embarrassment, as a sixteen-year-old he experienced a conversion and threw himself into evangelization work with the Salvation Army. He felt called to devote his life to telling others about Jesus. From then on, Eberhard's life would be marked by his uncompromising desire to live out the radical way of Christ.

Eberhard studied theology in Halle an der Saale, where in 1907 he met his future wife, Emmy von Hollander, a professor's daughter and member of the Baltic German aristocracy. It was love at first sight, a love only surpassed by their shared love for Jesus. Both of them participated enthusiastically in a revival movement then sweeping Germany, and through scripture became convinced of believer's baptism. When these convictions became known, Emmy's mother threatened suicide if Emmy, who had been baptized as a baby, was rebaptized, and Eberhard was barred from taking his doctoral examination in theology despite having already submitted his dissertation. Undeterred, both left the Lutheran state church. They received believer's baptism the following year, though without joining another denomination. Eberhard switched his studies to philosophy, receiving his PhD in 1909. The couple married immediately afterward.

Eberhard flung himself into evangelization and publishing work with the Student Christian Movement. But over the next few years, he became increasingly dissatisfied with the evangelical Christianity of Germany's "free churches," which seemed to focus unhealthily on personal salvation while avoiding the social implications of Jesus' demands in the Gospels, especially the Sermon on the Mount. Social injustice and the horrors of World War I only strengthened his conviction that discipleship demanded more than most Christians were giving. He also became convinced that a follower of Jesus must renounce all violence and participation in the coercive power of the state.

Germany was defeated in 1918, ending the "Great War." A succession of revolutions swept Europe the following year. Eberhard and Emmy began hosting discussion evenings in their Berlin townhouse to seek answers in Jesus' teachings to the turbulent times they found themselves in. Through this search they felt a call to give up everything to follow Christ more faithfully. They moved from Berlin to the remote village of Sannerz. There, with a handful of like-minded Christians, they began to live in community of goods after the example of the first church in Jerusalem. Thousands of guests would come in the next years, and though most would move on, more than a few stayed. The community relocated to a nearby farm, and its ranks gradually swelled to more than a hundred. Inspired by the sixteenth-century Hutterites, they adopted the name Bruderhof, or "place of brothers."

In 1929, Eberhard, whose appreciation for the witness of the early Hutterites had only deepened after a decade of communal living, made contact with their descendants living in North America. He traveled across the Atlantic to live among them for a year, and in December 1930 was ordained as a minister by all branches of the Hutterian church and given responsibility for the German Bruderhof and for mission in Europe.

Trouble began not long after Adolf Hitler's rise to power in 1933. On hearing the news that President Hindenburg had appointed Hitler as chancellor, Eberhard remarked: "The president has no idea what demons he is conjuring up." Branded as communists, the community became a target for official hostility almost immediately. Eberhard and the other members refused to use the *Heil Hitler* greeting or fly the swastika flag. In meetings of the community and its guests, Eberhard denounced National Socialism as "tyrannical despotism" and "a movement in absolute opposition to the cross." His rejection of anti-Semitism and racism included welcoming people of Jewish, Romani, and non-European descent into the community.

The Nazis solidified their power quickly over the following weeks, through the targeting of Jewish businesses, the Reichstag fire, and the Enabling Act, which gave Hitler the powers of a dictator. Local harassment of the Bruderhof escalated too, with house searches by the police, boycotts of its goods, and threats by neighbors with Nazi sympathies. On Good Friday, 1933, the community gathered to discuss what to do. Emmy said, "We must know exactly what is actually happening. Nothing is being written about it. . . . Now the Jews are being persecuted; next it will be the Christians."

"It is urgently necessary for us to make perfectly clear to the authorities why we live as we do and what our purpose is. Hitler says terrible things in his speeches," another member added.

Eberhard expressed what they were all feeling when he said, "We want to put all our efforts into building up this place, as long as we have it, as a memorial to God's honor. To our last moment here we want to do the very utmost that can be done. . . . We shall stay firmly in this place that was shown to us until God sends us a direct call to leave it. . . . I believe it is possible to speak very plainly to this government. So we must ask God that an interview will be possible and that we are granted a completely frank exchange."

During that summer and fall Eberhard repeatedly visited various offices in the regional government to get information and gain sympathy for the community's cause. On October 27 he had a difficult meeting with a certain Dr. Stachels, who told him of an upcoming mandatory national vote in which the German people would be called upon to affirm Hitler's policies. The Nazi official told him: "If you don't say yes, Dr. Arnold, there is only one thing left – concentration camp."

Shaken by this exchange, Eberhard returned from Fulda by taxi, but walked the last stretch by foot, as usual. Walking in the dark on treacherous terrain, he slipped and suffered a compound fracture of his leg. Brought to his house in considerable pain, Eberhard immediately gathered the community to report about his day. As one of his sons recalled:

> He told us about the dismal answer he had received from the Nazi official, and that non-participation in the forthcoming vote would mean concentration camp. He was in great pain, but he spoke to us with fiery love to strengthen the faith of us all, so that all might be ready to hold out through need and maybe even death right to the end. To gain time he suggested that we should go to the voting, but that everyone should write the same statement, namely that we recognize the government but have a different calling from Christ.

Two days later, Eberhard addressed the community again, reminding them that God might call on them to give the same sacrifice
offered by the early Christian and early Anabaptist martyrs:

> The deepest need we have to fear is by no means the need of being
> persecuted, however difficult it will be when outward hardships
> are laid upon us. The deepest need is when fear overcomes a person,
> fear that he might become weak in the face of persecution. For this
> fear tells him that he is already losing his firm connection with
> God. So in these difficult, uncertain times it is essential that in the
> face of the threatening danger we find the wisdom that prevents
> fear from overcoming us. . . . In silent devotion we want to hold
> ourselves ready for whatever God wants to do with us.

With the vote looming, Eberhard wrote in the name of the
community to Hitler himself. The letter made clear that though
the Bruderhof members respected the government as having been
set over them by God, they would not acknowledge Hitler as their
Führer since their allegiance belonged first and foremost to the true
"leader [*Führer*] and liberator" – Jesus Christ. Eberhard concluded
his letter with a prayer for Hitler's conversion "from being a historical instrument as a wielder of supreme state authority to being an
ambassador of the humiliated Christ."

On the day of the national vote, all Bruderhof members went to
the polls as required. But rather than voting yes or no, they affixed
a handwritten sticker on their ballots that read:

> By conviction and will, I am pledged to the gospel and the disci-
> pleship of Jesus Christ, the coming kingdom of God, and the love
> and unity of his church. This is the one and only vocation God
> has given me as my calling. Out of this faith I intercede before
> God and all people for my fatherland and above all for the Reich
> government as men with another and different vocation, which
> is not mine, but a vocation given by God to my beloved rulers
> Hindenburg and Hitler.

This radical statement did not pass unnoticed. Four days after the vote, the Bruderhof was surrounded by 140 Gestapo and storm troopers. Emmy recalled:

> No one was allowed to leave his room or place of work, and at every door stood one of these men. Then they pushed their way into the rooms and searched everything. . . . They searched longest in Eberhard's study, in the archives, and in the library, looking for writings "hostile to the state." Eberhard himself lay on the sofa with his newly-operated leg, while these people pushed their way in and searched. They probably would have liked to take Eberhard away at that time and put him in a concentration camp. But what could they do with this sick man? Late that evening a big car drove off loaded with books, writings and records.

After the raid, persecution of the Bruderhof intensified. In December 1933 the school district superintendent, formerly a good friend, came to test the Bruderhof pupils to see if they had been "patriotically instructed" as required. After finding the children completely unfamiliar with Nazi ideology, he ordered them to sing a Nazi song. The children were silent. As a consequence, the school was ordered closed, and the superintendent arranged for Nazi teachers to be sent after Christmas to take over the children's education.

In response, Eberhard arranged for all the school-age children to leave Germany soon after New Year. Eventually, they were all reunited in a newly rented property in the principality of Liechtenstein, perched at a 4800-foot elevation. Here a new school was started, with a community to support it. Over the next two years, Eberhard would make repeated trips up the rugged Alpine road, in winter going on crutches for the last half mile, often through knee-deep snow. His leg had never healed properly.

In March 1935 Hitler announced the introduction of compulsory military conscription, effective April 1. The penalty for non-compliance was death. All German males of military age in the community left Germany for Liechtenstein before the deadline. Although this ensured their safety temporarily, they could not reenter the country, and their sudden departure dealt a heavy blow to the community's farm, publishing, and handcraft businesses.

By May 1935 Eberhard was having increased discomfort in his leg. Emmy was concerned that it was becoming more crooked. For the last half year, he had been suffering from persistent swelling and pain, inadequate bone healing, and heartbeat irregularity. He was hospitalized briefly, but soon the pressing need to lead the community and protect it from Nazi persecution put him on his feet again.

By now, the Bruderhof was not only impoverished by local boycotts, but isolated. Eberhard's attempts to join forces with other Christians who rejected National Socialism had met with mixed success. Dietrich Bonhoeffer had responded warmly, and friendships forged with Dutch Mennonites and Quakers would later prove crucial. But most German Christians he approached – including the Pastors' Emergency League and even prominent German Anabaptists – were wary of the Bruderhof's refusal to bear arms, arguing that it was their obligation according to Romans 13 to serve in Hitler's army. Martin Niemöller, the courageous anti-Nazi pastor who would later gain fame as a survivor of the concentration camps, was typical. When Eberhard sent representatives to his house to ask for solidarity, he refused even to shake their hands, declaring: "I am proud to have served as a U-boat commander in the last war. If Hitler calls me back to my post, I will go."

Meanwhile, Eberhard, accompanied by his son, traveled throughout England for three months to raise funds. He could not afford the time for further medical care, and spent the summer and fall shuttling between Germany, Liechtenstein, and Switzerland to hold the scattered community together, raise money, and deal with official attempts to close the Bruderhof down. Alarmed at the worsening condition of Eberhard's leg, Emmy contacted Dr. Paul Zander, a surgeon in Darmstadt and longtime friend. An appointment was scheduled for November 13, 1935.

In the days before his admission to the hospital, Eberhard spent much time preparing a series of talks on the history of the early Anabaptists and other Christian groups. His wife recalled: "He was tremendously lively, full of enthusiasm over the working of God in history. He spoke to the community for hours, full of inner fire and a deep movement of heart. How much he longed that something of this might awaken again in our circle!" From the hospital in Darmstadt, Eberhard wrote to his wife:

> How small in itself is the life of an individual; how small is the family life of husband and wife with their children; how small also the circle of friends who feel drawn to each other on a personal level; how small are the individual work areas like the kitchen or the sewing room or the office; and finally, how small is the Bruderhof with all its little souls!
>
> But how great are God and his kingdom! How great is the historical hour of world crisis, of world suffering, and world catastrophe; and how much greater still is God's hour of world judgment and Christ's hour of coming redemption! How burning should be our longing to learn more and more about all these things, to go deeper and deeper, to have an interest in them. And how ardently we should expect and long for the Day itself, the coming Day, the liberating and uniting Day!

When Dr. Zander examined Eberhard, he urged that surgical intervention to reset the bone be carried out at once. The operation, which took place on November 16, revealed that Eberhard's leg had been mercilessly overused during the previous two years; not only had the fracture failed to heal, but the bone marrow and surrounding tissue were infected. An amputation would be necessary.

Wednesday, November 20, was a national holiday, Repentance Day. Though by now Eberhard was mostly unconscious, he awoke and called out loudly so that others heard: "Have Hitler and Goebbels repented?"

The surgery to amputate took place at noon two days later. Though the operation only took ten minutes, Eberhard never recovered consciousness and died at four o'clock that afternoon. His body was taken home to the Bruderhof for burial.

Eberhard's words in 1934 sum up his attitude toward one of the most oppressive governments in history:

> The apostle Paul says that we are ambassadors of God, representing Christ, the messiah king, the regent of the last kingdom (2 Cor. 5:20). When the British ambassador is in the British embassy in Berlin, he is not subject to the laws of Germany. The grounds of the embassy are inviolable. In the residence of the ambassador, only the laws of the country he represents are valid. We are ambassadors of the kingdom of God. This means that we do nothing at all except what the king of God's kingdom would himself do for his kingdom. When we take this service upon ourselves we enter into mortal danger.

Two years after Eberhard's death, one morning at dawn, the community was again surrounded by the Gestapo and police. This time the purpose of the raid was no longer to investigate. The Bruderhof was dissolved, its assets confiscated, and its directors arrested. (They were released two months later.) The other members were transported out of the country by bus, and were given temporary refuge by Mennonites in the Netherlands. Eventually, new Bruderhof communities would be founded in England and Paraguay and, after the war, in the United States, Germany, and Australia. Through the continuing life of the church community he founded, Eberhard's work and witness live on after him.

22

Johann Kornelius Martens

died 1938 (assumed), in Zaporizhia, Ukraine

JOHANN KORNELIUS MARTENS didn't set out to become a pastor. A young man of German descent, he was a schoolteacher in the Ukrainian village of Michaelsburg, and later in the towns of Dobas and Einlage. These communities were largely populated by German Mennonites who had moved to the Ukraine. The late 1700s and early 1800s had seen an influx of immigrants seeking land and religious liberty in this fertile agricultural region. But the following century saw major political and cultural upheaval in Europe. Even in the Ukraine, rapid industrialization and militarization would not leave the religious and peaceable Mennonites untouched.

In 1897, Johann married Katharina Janzen. The couple had fourteen children, though six of them died as infants. Katharina died in 1921. Soon after, Johann married Maria Peters, a widow who already had four children of her own. Johann struggled to support his large household, even though he was now the educational district head of his region.

At one point, Johann was pursued by a band of anarchist fighters loyal to Nestor Makhno, whose anti-bourgeois attacks particularly singled out prosperous Mennonite landowners. As Johann fled on foot by night to a nearby town, he promised God that if his life was spared he would accept a call to the ministry. He escaped successfully.

In 1917 his congregation in the community of Konsweide elected him as preacher. In 1924 he was elected elder. Johann also took over his parents' farm to supplement his meager income.

But conditions for Mennonites in the Ukraine worsened rapidly. The repressive Marxist regime was extending its influence into rural areas, and anti-German sentiment grew. Many thousands of Mennonites who were able to make the journey emigrated to North America.

Though Johann was eager to serve his congregation and the Mennonites of his region, accepting the position of elder had not been easy. Answering the call to ministry meant choosing hardship and possible danger for himself and his family. At the time, all preachers had to register with the government and relinquish their right to vote.

In 1925, Johann went as a delegate to the Mennonite general conference in Moscow, a gathering that would later be called the "Second Martyrs' Synod of the Anabaptists." Of the eighty-six delegates present at the conference, only eighteen would make it to safety in North America. Over the next sixteen years, all the rest would be imprisoned and either banished or killed by the communist government. (Two of Johann's married daughters did manage to emigrate to Canada, but Johann and the rest of the family could not follow because one of his daughters, Kaethe, was physically disabled, making her ineligible to immigrate to the United States or Canada.)

Johann returned from the conference and continued to shepherd his flock. But increasingly, expressions of religion were curbed or banned. Taxes on pastors were gradually increased until they could no longer afford to feed their families. Johann paid the levy faithfully as long as he could; when he could no longer pay, the congregation scraped together the amount needed to pay the tax on his behalf. Yet it was clear that the government's goal was to make it practically impossible to worship or hold a position of religious authority. Johann knew that even if he paid the tax, he would eventually be banned.

The growing persecution soon came into the open. In 1929, the government forced Johann and his family out of their home. They were able to remain in the village only a short time before the authorities loaded them on a truck and took them to the town of Kronsweide, where they were able to stay with relatives. But this didn't last long. The following year, the local village council voted to ban Johann once again, on the grounds that he was a member of the bourgeoisie and held anti-Soviet views. He and his family were moved to Neuenburg, where they were given a small amount of infertile land outside the village. Although they planted vegetables and potatoes, they were not allowed to harvest them.

Then came the night of June 27, 1931. Johann, Maria, and two of their youngest children were packed into railroad cars with two thousand other people and banished to the harsh Ural region. During the ten-day journey the deportees often sang the song "Befiehl du deine Wege." The final verse is a powerful prayer:

Make an end, O Lord, make an end
of all our distress,
strengthen our feet and hands,
and until our death
at all times let us feel your
care and faithfulness,

and so go on our way
with confidence to heaven.

They fought fiercely to survive during their exile in the vast Ural forests. The two children had to join in the backbreaking work, cutting down trees and hauling logs. Eight months into their time in the Urals, fifteen-year-old Lydia escaped.

Johann and Maria's older children, who had not been exiled, sent supply packages to their parents. But when this was discovered by the government, the Martens family was moved to another, undisclosed location.

There, too, conditions were terrible. At night they were forced to shelter under an upturned boat. The aging Johann nearly died from heart and kidney conditions, greatly exacerbated by poor nutrition and the physical stress of his job unloading heavy sacks. He was transferred to an easier job herding horses, but his health continued to deteriorate. Eventually he saw a doctor, who against orders issued a certificate declaring Johann unfit to remain in his current job. He was thus transferred again, this time to a bookkeeping position in the labor camp's office. Meanwhile, his community back home petitioned the government for the family's release, but to no avail.

So they struggled on. To provide for the family, Maria had to walk twenty kilometers to collect food supplies, including heavy sacks of potatoes. As she arrived back home from one of these journeys, a jolt of pain shot up her spine. From that point on, the entire right side of her body was paralyzed.

After five years of grueling work, Maria's paralysis and Johann's age and worsening condition gained them their freedom. In 1936 they were allowed to return home to Einlage, though their son had to stay in the camp. When they arrived home, no house remained. Friends loaned them 3,000 rubles to purchase half of a house for the family. Johann worked wherever he could during the day and served as watchman at a collective horse barn at night. He also did the household work, since Maria was unable. Their children supported them as well. With their combined income, they survived and slowly paid back their house loan.

In 1938, trouble struck again. Johann, two of his sons, and his son-in-law were arrested as political criminals and imprisoned in the city of Zaporizhia. The remaining family members received mixed reports of their situation, but were unable to send aid, see them, or confirm details of their condition. Some were told they had been exiled to the far north; others, that Johann had died.

One of Johann's sons and his son-in-law were shot in Zaporizhia in October. Johann and his other son were never heard from again. It is likely that they were shot as well, a fate that befell 80 percent of Germans arrested in the region in the late 1930s.

Years later, Kaethe, Johann's crippled daughter, recorded the story of the family's travails. "Every inquiry has proven useless," she wrote of her fruitless search for her father and brother. "In ten years we have found no trace of them." Kaethe and her mother were eventually able to find security living with Lydia, the daughter who had escaped from the Urals, and her husband.

Whether Johann went to a slow death in Siberia or to an immediate death before a communist firing squad, his witness as a leader of his people in the face of intense persecution remains.

23

Ahn Ei Sook

persecuted from 1939 to 1945, in Korea

BEGINNING WITH the Japan-Korea Treaty of 1876, Japan began integrating Korea into its empire. In 1910, Japan officially annexed Korea, ending the ancient Joseon dynasty. This had a profound impact on all aspects of Korean life, including religion.

Japanese authorities demolished 85 percent of the buildings of the historic Gyeongbokgung compound in Korea's capital, Seoul, including the primary palace that had for centuries been a national symbol. The Japanese General Government Building was constructed in its place. Japanese Shinto-style golden horns were added near the roof of Sungnyemun, one of eight gates in the wall surrounding Seoul, turning a symbol of Korean pride into a quasi-Japanese monument.

During the 1930s the Japanese attempted to solidify Korean loyalty by requiring all Korean citizens to participate in State

Shinto worship practices. On the first of each month, the Japanese forced Koreans to gather around a shrine of Japan's sun goddess and bow down in worship.

This was an especially difficult command for the students and faculty of the Christian school where Ahn Ei Sook taught music. When the girls were summoned to gather in the playground for the monthly trek to the Japanese shrine, many hid in classrooms and restrooms, hoping to avoid worshipping at the shrine. But it was no use. The principal commanded teachers to find the children and bring them out.

As Ei Sook watched teachers move from room to room collecting students, she was filled with sadness. She wanted to cry, but could not. She closed the door, fell on her knees, and silently prayed to Jesus.

"Miss Ahn! Are you there?" It was the principal's voice, muffled through the closed door. She had come to escort Ei Sook to the shrine. The music teacher opened the door to face her superior. "Today is the first of the month," the principal said. "We have to take the girls up the mountain to the shrine. Remember?"

Ei Sook stood silently, staring in defiance. "You are not the only believer," said the principal. "This is a Christian school. Most of the pupils are Christians. So are all the other teachers. I too am a Christian. Think about it, Miss Ahn. Is there any believer in Christ who wants to bow to heathen gods? We all hate to do such a thing, but we Christians are being persecuted by a power too ruthless to stand against. Unless we worship at the Japanese shrine, they will close this school!"

Ei Sook knew that the pressure to conform was great. Anyone whom the Japanese authorities found unwilling to bow before their shrines was branded a traitor. They were tortured. Christians across Korea had died because they would not give up their faith. Ei Sook pitied her principal, who was responsible for the welfare of the students, the teachers, and the school itself. If anyone did not show up to worship, all would be put in danger. It was a heavy load to bear.

Still, Ei Sook could not see how her superior could cast aside the Lord she claimed to follow. The music teacher didn't budge. "You can see what great trouble you will cause this school if you fail to cooperate," the principal said, a mixture of fear and hatred in her voice. "But you don't seem to care about that. You are thinking only of yourself."

Finally, Ei Sook answered, "If you want me to go to the mountain, I will."

The principal led her out of her classroom and down the stairs toward the playground. "And you will worship at the shrine, Miss Ahn. Right?"

The music teacher didn't answer. As she walked past her students, she thought she could see their faces turn to dismay. "Even Miss Ahn is going," one girl said. "Now God will surely turn away from us!" Another said, "Our principal has such power! She has made Miss Ahn go to the shrine." All Ei Sook could do was pray. *O Lord,* she prayed, *I am so weak! But I am your sheep, so I must obey and follow you. Lord, watch over me.*

The students and teachers started up the mountain. They fell in line with the large crowd gathering before the Japanese shrine. Ei Sook could feel her heart beating. A voice called out, "Attention!" and the gathered Koreans straightened their backs. Then the voice said, "Our profoundest bow to Amaterasu Omikami [the sun goddess]!" Everyone gathered before the shrine bent their upper bodies in a deep, uniform bow. All but one.

Ahn Ei Sook stood upright, her face tilted toward the sky. A moment before, she had been filled with guilt and fear. Now she was overcome by a feeling of calm. Inside her head, a voice told her, *You have fulfilled your responsibility.* She heard a murmur pass through the crowd as those bowed around her realized she had not joined them. Walking away from the shrine, she thought, *I am dead. Ahn Ei Sook died today at Mount Namsan.* She did not fear death, but the thought of torture caused her to shudder.

Seeking safety, she fled. But after months in hiding, in March 1939 Ei Sook decided to go to Tokyo to appeal to the Japanese authorities for the persecuted Christians of Korea. She was promptly arrested and spent the next six years in prison. Her disobedience was punished severely, but in the filth and brutality of prison, she shared the gospel with her fellow prisoners. Later she said, "I cannot explain how such a weak woman as I was given such wonderful blessings during times of fear and suffering."

The Japanese administration of Korea ended in 1945, when Japan was defeated at the end of World War II. The Japanese shrines were burned. In 1940, thirty-four Christians including Ahn Ei Sook had entered Pyongyang prison. On August 17, 1945, when they were finally released, only fourteen remained alive. One of them was Ahn Ei Sook.

As the prisoners made their way out, a sympathetic prison guard shouted, "Ladies and gentlemen! These are the ones who for six long years refused to worship Japanese gods. They fought against severe torture, hunger, and cold, and have won out without bowing their heads to the idol worship of Japan. Today they are the champions of the faith!" The gathered crowd greeted the prisoners as heroes, shouting, "Praise the name of Jesus!" and singing joyously:

All hail the power of Jesus' name
Let angels prostrate fall.
Bring forth the royal diadem,
And crown him Lord of all . . .

24

Jakob Rempel

died 1941, in Orel, USSR

JAKOB REMPEL came from a long line of Russian farmers, but his father decided to break with tradition by going into business and building a mill. The venture failed. Forced into bankruptcy, Jakob's father moved from one trade to another while his large family suffered great poverty. As a young boy, Jakob spent much of his time helping his mother care for his twelve siblings. This devotion to caring for others would carry on for the rest of his life.

Jakob flourished in the village school, but despite his intellectual gifts he became a stable boy for a local farmer. Still, although he was committed to supporting his family, he never lost his desire to learn and teach. Before long he was given an opportunity to educate others. A few Mennonites were placed in Jewish villages in Russia to demonstrate new farming methods, and these Mennonite families were allowed to educate their own children privately.

Since educators were hard to come by, Jakob was appointed as a teacher in one of these villages, even before he received the proper qualifications.

After a few years of teaching, Jakob received a scholarship from a wealthy mill owner to attend seminary in Basel, Switzerland for six years. When he returned to Russia, he held various teaching positions while simultaneously serving as a pastor of the Mennonite church in Ekaterinoslav. In 1920 he was appointed as a professor of German at the University of Moscow. That year he was also asked to serve as elder of the Neu-Chortitza Mennonite congregation. Because Jakob was even considering a religious office, the university removed him from professorship. Turned away from this hard-earned teaching position, he accepted the call to serve as elder and was ordained on May 2, 1920.

Two years later, Jakob was elected chairman of the church's Commission for Religious Affairs. In this new position, he represented the Mennonite churches of Russia in negotiations with the anti-religious communist government in Moscow. He fought to free young Mennonites from required military service, and did his best to preserve ties among Mennonite communities being persecuted by the government. Jakob also became a regular teacher at Bible conferences.

But conditions for believers in Russia were worsening. In response to severe persecutions, over five hundred members of the Neu-Chortitza church emigrated to America in 1923. Though he could have joined this steady stream of emigrants, Jakob decided to stay in Russia to serve his remaining congregants. In one letter, Jakob wrote, "For me, the community is the most important thing."

In 1925 Jakob led a Mennonite general conference in Moscow. Communist authorities took note of every person who attended the conference. Fearing for his family's safety, Jakob requested a less visible leadership position. Another man was appointed commissioner, but Jakob continued overseeing the projects he had started. Among these was the organization of an illegal seminary.

When Jakob was invited to attend the first Mennonite World Conference in Basel later that year to celebrate the 400th anniversary of the Mennonite Church, he was denied a Swiss visa. Not one to waste an opportunity, Jakob toured the Mennonite congregations of Germany instead. This gave him a picture of life away from Russian persecution, and many in his congregation feared he would leave for Germany permanently. But in a letter home Jakob wrote, "It is quite something to be outside of Russia. I think one could forget everything and begin life anew. But what of those suffering at home, what of the many large congregations! I'm drawn back there. Wife and children can be taken along, but not the congregation."

Although in theory Russian citizens were allowed to hold religious convictions, the government banned religious propaganda and applied pressure on church leaders. Preachers were forced to register as "religious servants," giving up their right to vote. They were also burdened with crippling taxes. As ministers followed their congregants from Russia to America, it became more and more difficult to find suitable replacements. The few qualified candidates remaining often declined to accept ministerial nominations. Still, Jakob refused to let the dangers deter him, and worked tirelessly to ensure that congregations were cared for.

Eventually the government pressure Jakob had long worked to spare others came to rest on his own shoulders. In fall of 1929, the government fined him 800 rubles for his religious work, though his annual income was less than 360 rubles. A month later a hearing was held, resulting in Jakob's expulsion from Grünfeld, where he lived at the time. Realizing that this would soon lead to his arrest, Jakob left the city and his family without saying goodbye to his congregation or neighbors. In response, the government seized his possessions, money, and home, driving his family out into the rain. They were forced to find shelter in a neighboring village.

Realizing that he could no longer lead his congregation, Jakob left for Moscow to seek emigration papers with a group of thousands of Mennonites. There, the GPU (the Soviet intelligence service and secret police) arrested him, accusing him of instigating the mass emigration from Russia.

Jakob served seven months in custody, charged with "anti-Soviet and counterrevolutionary activity." He was told that if he renounced his faith he could once again teach as a professor in the University of Moscow. Jakob refused. He was then sentenced to ten years of hard labor in a prison camp on the island of Solovki in the White Sea.

In prison Jakob experienced daily horrors. His room was covered with human excrement. Electric lights glared so brightly in his eyes that he nearly went blind. When he was transferred to another camp in 1932, he took advantage of a rare chance at escape. Jakob jumped from the train into a mound of snow.

Having gained his freedom, he fled to a Mennonite colony in Turkestan. For three days he ate nothing but snow. He contracted typhus. Eventually his oldest son, Alexander, located him in Turkestan, living under a tree, incoherent and nearly unconscious. When Alexander examined his father's injuries, he discovered that Jakob had no fingernails. During his time in prison, needles had been forced under his nails until they eventually fell out.

Jakob experienced peace as a free citizen for nearly four years, using the pseudonym of Sudermann (his wife's maiden name). During this period, he had time to reflect on his sufferings. He wrote the following:

> I rarely experience severe worries or troublesome thoughts. When I was taken out of my work in the past, separated from life, led into solitude, into suffering after suffering, when sicknesses alternated

and the end of one marked the beginning of another, then I asked myself what Jesus would say about this. When I was inwardly sure that Jesus would have kept silent as he kept silent in his suffering, then I not only became silent but loved silence above all else. In deep seclusion I endured the hard struggle without human help. God led me into suffering, men executed it. God, however, protected me and led me out.

In the spring of 1935 Jakob was able to visit his family. But the following year someone betrayed him, and he was arrested at Khiva. Once again the authorities accused him of "counter-revolutionary and anti-Soviet activity." They condemned him to death. But after he submitted a plea for grace, Jakob received a reduced sentence: ten years in prison, followed by five years with no civil rights. He was imprisoned in Vladimir, then moved to the state prison in Orel.

Until June of 1941, Jakob was allowed to write letters to his family. In one of his final letters, he wrote, "You can put me in chains, hit me, cut off my head, but no one can take my faith . . . away from me. From a stable boy to professor . . . and now [in jail] I'm at the pinnacle of my life."

That fall, as World War II raged, German troops pushed toward Orel. Soviet authorities were pressured to finalize the sentences of their prisoners. The Military Collegium of the USSR Supreme Court sentenced Jakob to death. He was shot on September 11, 1941, along with nearly 160 other prisoners.

Five years after Jakob's death, his son Alexander wrote: "[My father] has now left the stage of life. In eternity God will again place him on stage and we hope that the verse in Revelation 2:10 will apply, where we read: 'Be faithful, even to the point of death, and I will give you life as your victor's crown.'"

In 1989, nearly fifty years after his unjust execution, a resolution of the USSR Prosecutor's Office exonerated Jakob Rempel.

PART IV

Recent Witnesses

25

Clarence Jordan

persecuted from 1943 to 1957, in Georgia,
United States

"Rev. Clarence L. Jordan Dead; Led Interracial Farm Project," reads a brief obituary in the *New York Times* of October 31, 1969. The article lists the customary details of birth, marriage, family, and death. Less usual are the clipped mentions of his work, including the farm project alluded to in the title, with references to a Southern vernacular translation of the Bible and an agricultural religious community practicing Christian brotherhood.

Between those few lines lies a remarkable story of faith and persecution. Clarence was born July 29, 1912, to prominent white citizens of Talbotton, Georgia. The American South of his youth was one of racial segregation and prejudice. Even as a boy, Clarence was sensitive to the rampant hypocrisy evidenced by such injustices, particularly when they intersected religion in Bible-belt Georgia.

At age twelve, Clarence joined a local church after a summer revival. But during Sunday school he wondered why, if their song – "Red and yellow, black and white, they are precious in his sight; Jesus loves the little children of the world" – was true, all the little black children in his neighborhood were treated so poorly.

As a boy, Clarence's bedroom window looked out on the Talbot County Jail, only a hundred yards off. Coming home from school, he would stop by the prison yard, where he befriended the cook and the chain gang workers. From them, he learned about "the stretcher," a frame used to fasten a man's feet to the floor while his arms were pulled toward the ceiling by a block and tackle. It was a torture used almost exclusively on black men.

New at the church, Clarence listened one evening as the prison warden, a bass in the choir, regaled the congregation with "Love Lifted Me." That night Clarence was woken by moans of suffering from the prison. "He knew not only who was on the stretcher," commented a biographer, "but who was pulling the ropes – the same man who only hours before had sung his heart out to God. 'That nearly tore me to pieces,' Clarence reflected years later."

In 1929, hoping to improve farming techniques for poor share-croppers, Clarence enrolled at the University of Georgia's College of Agriculture. He joined the Reserve Officers Training Corps (ROTC) and went through several years of military training. But in the summer of 1933, days away from earning his commission, he came to a crisis of conscience during a training event. With pistol and saber in hand, he charged on horseback through the Georgia forest, hacking and shooting at training dummies. As he rode, Christ's words from the Sermon on the Mount, which Clarence had been memorizing, haunted him: "But I say to you, love your enemies..." He dismounted, approached the officer in charge, and resigned his commission.

By this time, Clarence had come to feel that spiritual poverty was as pressing an issue as economic poverty. He decided to enroll in the Southern Baptist Theological Seminary in Kentucky. During his studies, he fell in love with his future wife, Florence. He warned her that she shouldn't marry him if she "wanted to be the wife of an important preacher at a First Baptist Church." The warning, which proved well warranted, did not dissuade her.

After Clarence's graduation and the couple's marriage in 1936, their concern for racial justice and radical Christian living continued to deepen. Clarence served inner-city congregations, began teaching New Testament at Simmons University (an African-American seminary in Louisville), served a Baptist mission association, and, with his flair for language, received a doctorate in New Testament Greek at the age of twenty-six. He was always ready to discuss his passions – especially nonviolence and the radical sharing of resources – none of which were likely to lead to an easy life for a Christian in the South.

In 1941 Clarence met former missionary Martin England, a man who shared many of his convictions. They began dreaming together, combining deep concern over the agricultural crisis following the Great Depression with the belief that the Sermon on the Mount could be a guide for practical life, not merely an unattainable ideal. With a great deal of faith, though few resources, the two began searching for land. A few miles southwest of Americus, Georgia, they found the acreage that was to become Koinonia Farm, *koinonia* being the Greek word used in Acts to refer to the earliest gatherings of Christians. The property consisted of 440 acres of bleak land, eroded and ugly. The farmhouse was uninhabitable. "This is it," Clarence announced after a thorough inspection.

After acquiring funds for the down payment for Koinonia, through a well-timed gift of the precise amount they lacked, the Jordan and England families began the backbreaking process of building their vision. The farm's outbuildings sagged and the fences were down. The dilapidated farmhouse was in such disrepair that after a new chicken coop was built, Florence expressed her desire to move into it rather than the house.

While Clarence and Martin did the much-needed repairs, their families stayed elsewhere until the farmhouse was, in Florence's words, "at least campable." During this time they carefully observed neighbors to pick up on local farming techniques, and, in one of the first in a series of bold moves against the entrenched segregation of the area, brought in a local sharecropper as hired help. They ate their meals together, white and black – a practice which didn't escape the notice of the locals.

News got around. One evening, the farm was visited by the Ku Klux Klan. "We don't allow the sun to set on anybody who eats with niggers," their leader said. Sunset was approaching. Clarence looked at it and thought fast. Then, with the humor that diffused so many other tense interactions throughout his ministry, he shook the man's hand vigorously. "Why, I'm a Baptist preacher," he said. "I've heard about people who had power over the sun, but I never hoped to meet one." The man began laughing. The sun set without incident.

Speaking years later of the dangers he faced at this time, Clarence didn't downplay the risks involved. "We knew white men could disappear, just like black men. It scared us, but the alternative was not to do it, and that scared us more."

The farm was beginning to be successful. Poultry and eggs became a profitable venture for Koinonia, and Clarence shared his knowledge of production with other farmers eager to establish thriving flocks. He put his innovator's mind to work designing the first mobile peanut harvester. A lending "cow library" ensured that locals in need of milk could borrow an animal at no cost.

The once-bare acreage was becoming fruitful, and the farm grew. But Koinonia quickly became known for much more than produce. It became a haven for diverse people – from conscientious objectors seeking a positive alternative to war as World War

II dragged on, to local black neighbors who found not just sympathetic white people running the farm, but people willing to shake their hand, share a table, and live with them as family.

As the months passed by, the farm's radical values of peacemaking, shared resources, and love for all people proved to have founded an effective working community. But the growth – and the fact that the farm wasn't merely drying up and blowing away, as some had hoped it would – brought even fiercer opposition.

Rehoboth Baptist Church, home to several members of Koinonia, made it clear (after the Koinonia folks brought a dark-skinned student from India to a worship service) that farm members were no longer welcome. Clarence handed a Bible to a deacon in the church delegation sent to inform him of this decision, and offered to apologize to the church if the deacon could point out the offense. The deacon flung it down. "Don't give me any of this Bible stuff!"

"I'm asking you to give it to me," Clarence said. The meeting didn't end pleasantly. Later, an old Rehoboth deacon asked Clarence to forgive him for his vote to ban Koinonia's members from their church. Clarence forgave him, urged him to stay at Rehoboth, and exulted later that the man was a "divine irritant" in the church until he died.

By 1952 the farm was supporting forty-one people, twenty-two of them children. In 1954, the desegregation of schools caused profound turmoil in the South, heightening already simmering racial tensions and bringing overt persecution from white groups toward the little community, starting with threatening phone calls and letters. By 1956 Koinonia's enemies had turned to destruction of key machinery and crops, and eventually outright violence. At the county level, officials used political leverage to put a stop to the farm's summer camp for black and white inner-city children. The solicitor general called for "the right kind of Klan to start up again and use a buggy whip on some of these race mixers." Koinonia was the clear target of his hatred.

Koinonia's roadside market was dynamited. A few days after the bombing, Koinonia Farm published an open letter in the newspaper, outlining their principles of nonviolence and inviting visitors to come to the farm. By way of reply, the local community boycotted them, refusing to buy any products or sell them goods. It was a tremendous blow. Then, the night after Christmas, a bullet shattered the farm's gas pump. On New Year's Day the perpetrators shot directly at the houses. For a week and a half the community wrestled with the question of whether to leave or stay. In spite of the danger and the urging of friends to abandon the operation, they decided to stay. "We knew we wouldn't be the first Christians to die," said Florence, "and we wouldn't be the last."

The deep faith reflected in this decision did not come without struggle. In a letter written in 1959, Clarence outlined the battle to love in spite of the tremendous opposition. He told a friend what he had felt on seeing the bombed roadside market:

> We could see the fiery glow, and this ignited a burning in my heart. I was scorched with anger, and I'm sure if I had known who had committed the act, there would have been considerable hatred in my heart. . . . The culprits have destroyed *our* property, I thought. And I hated their guts. Later I had the same reaction when various ones, including myself and my children, were shot at. The so-and-so's were trying to take *our* lives from us! The solution to this soul-destroying condition came only upon the recognition that neither property nor lives were ours but God's. They had never really been ours in any sense of the word. . . . And if this was how he wanted to spend his property and his people in order to accomplish his purposes, why should we pitch a tantrum?

There were other reasons to stay. Clarence spoke of the redemptive power of nursing health back into abused soil, and the pleasures of working the ground in community. His ideal of love for enemies flared brightly once again. "Shall we go off and leave them without hope?" he said in one interview. "We have too many enemies to leave them. The redemptive love of God must somehow break through. If it costs us our lives, if we must be hung on a cross to redeem our brothers and sisters in the flesh, so let it be. It will be well worth it."

This conviction continued to be tested, with ambushes by shotgun-toting vigilantes on remote roads, and a second bombing of the farm's market that left it completely destroyed. As the building and nearby farmland burned after the explosion, over forty spectators, including police, stood idly by.

Appeals to federal authorities fell on hard hearts. Clarence wrote directly to President Eisenhower, pleading for help; the president replied that Koinonia's protection was the responsibility of local authorities – the same ones who were subjecting the farm to investigations for "subversive activities" and "conspiracy to overthrow the government." A later investigation of Koinonia brought no indictment, but produced a sixteen-page report accusing the farm of being a communist operation and destroying its own property in a plot to get attention.

Meanwhile, the threats and violence grew. One night, machine guns peppered a car in which two members were keeping watch with flashlights. Tracer bullets fired into a home ignited a house curtain. A visitor's hat on a bedside stand was torn by a bullet. Koinonia's enemies even fired shots at the children as they played on the volleyball court, and at Clarence as he drove his tractor. The Ku Klux Klan converged on the farm and burned crosses. An arsonist threw a pillow soaked in gasoline into the home of longtime black farmhand Alma Jackson's mother, burning down the house. And all this time, the crippling boycott continued. Prompted by conscience, the owner of a feed store chain ordered his Americus store to serve Koinonia. The storefront was bombed within the week, with such explosive power that four neighboring buildings were damaged.

In spite of the opposition, people around the country expressed solidarity. A prominent Baptist pastor, Will D. Campbell, visited in support, as did a key leader of the Southern Baptist Convention. Dorothy Day, the founder of the Catholic Worker movement, came to the farm, took a midnight turn on watch duty, and was shot at for the first time in her life. After the insurance company would no longer cover the farm, people around the country pledged support. An idea to ship produce out via mail led to a popular movement to purchase Koinonia pecans around the country, with the slogan, "Help us ship the nuts out of Georgia."

Millard Fuller, a successful businessman and millionaire, visited Clarence and declared that conversations with him were like "a year, or two years, in seminary." Fuller decided to give away his wealth to the poor and move to Koinonia. His collaboration with Clarence to provide low-income housing eventually evolved into Habitat for Humanity, a global organization.

All the while, the Sermon on the Mount continued to fuel Clarence's message. From those chapters of the Gospel of Matthew, which he referred to as "the platform of the God Movement," he drew a profound critique of materialism, ecclesiasticism, and militarism, which he saw as the most powerful forces competing for people's minds and hearts. He had no respect for ostentatious Christianity or the self-righteous religiosity so rampant in Southern Christian culture. "That cross alone cost us ten thousand dollars," bragged a pastor as he gave Clarence a tour of his church.

"Time was, you could get them for nothing," Clarence shot back.

A sharp scholar who would read to congregations directly from his Greek New Testament, translating as he went, Clarence began to tell the gospel stories in images from the South, delighting his hearers with what would eventually become *The Cotton Patch Gospel*. The newborn Jesus was laid in an apple box, Simon Bar-Jonah became "Rock Johnson," and the prejudiced Jews and Gentiles of St. Paul's time became white and black neighbors of his own. "Well, the Idea became a man and moved in with us," he translated John 1. "Moving in" had become, in spite of all opposition, his own way of following Jesus.

In October of 1969, Clarence died of a heart attack in his writing shed at Koinonia Farm. The coroner refused to come to the farm, so Millard Fuller put his body in a station wagon and drove him into town. He was buried in a simple cedar box on a hill near the community he had founded on the gospel and a few acres of barren land.

Clarence's legacy, which lives on in Koinonia Farm, in Habitat for Humanity, and in his writings, can be summed up with one of his best-known statements: "Faith is not belief in spite of the evidence, but a life in scorn of the consequences."

26

Richard and Sabina Wurmbrand

persecuted from 1948 to 1964, in Romania

In 1936, Richard Wurmbrand married Sabina Oster. Two years later, they began following Jesus as the Messiah. Both had been raised in Jewish families, but thanks in part to the witness of a Christian carpenter named Christian Wölfkes, they joined the Anglican Mission to the Jews in their home city of Bucharest, Romania. Growing in spiritual maturity and passion, Richard was ordained in the Anglican Church. The couple quickly began a powerful ministry, one much needed during the horrors of World War II.

As a result of the nonaggression pact between Soviet and Nazi governments in 1939, Romania was pressured to join the Axis military campaign. German forces soon occupied the country, and Romania became the Third Reich's main source of oil. Richard and Sabina saw the violence and displacement as an opportunity for ministry and evangelism. They rescued Jewish children from dangerous ghettos and preached to Romanians hiding in the bomb shelters.

The Romanian population grew discontented with their German occupiers. The nation's King Michael led a coup d'état against Romania's Axis government in August of 1944, and Romania aligned itself with the Allies. In May 1945 German forces were defeated, and in August Japan surrendered, ending the war.

The war had taken a great toll on the Wurmbrands. Richard and Sabina had been captured and beaten numerous times. Sabina's entire family had been killed in Nazi concentration camps.

After the war, the German occupation was replaced by the Soviet Army. Richard and Sabina continued their ministry to their fellow Romanians and to the occupying forces. They joined the Lutheran Church, where Richard was ordained as a minister. They distributed over a million copies of the four Gospels to Russian soldiers in Romania, cleverly disguising the scriptures as communist propaganda. They also smuggled copies into Russia, the heart of the Soviet Union.

The new Romanian communist government, seeking to consolidate loyalty and rein in people of faith, organized a "Congress of Cults." The gathering was attended by various religious leaders, including the Wurmbrands. One by one, in impassioned speeches, these leaders swore loyalty to the government. They extolled the virtues of communism, despite its clear attempts to control and even suppress churches.

Richard and Sabina were disgusted by the actions of their fellow leaders. Sabina said, "Richard, stand up and wash away this shame from the face of Christ." Richard replied, "If I do, you'll lose your husband." But Sabina said what Richard knew in his heart: "I don't wish to have a coward as a husband." Richard stood up in front of the four thousand delegates as so many had done before him.

But instead of praising communism, he bravely declared that the church's duty is to glorify God and Christ alone.

On February 29, 1948, on his way to a church service, Richard was seized by the secret police and locked away in solitary confinement. For three years, he was confined to an underground cell with no lights or windows, where absolute silence was preserved – itself a form of sensory deprivation torture. The guards did not speak within earshot, and they wore felt on their shoes so that Richard could not even hear their steps.

After his release, in a document preparing readers to serve in the underground church, Richard wrote:

> We were drugged, we were beaten. I forgot my whole theology. I forgot the whole Bible. One day I observed that I had forgotten the "Our Father." I could not say it anymore. I knew that it began with "Our Father . . . ," but I did not know the continuation. I just kept happy and said, "Our Father, I have forgotten the prayer, but you surely know it by heart." . . . For a time my prayers were, "Jesus, I love you." And then after a little time again, "Jesus, I love you. Jesus, I love you." Then it became too difficult even to say this because we were doped. . . . The highest form of prayer that I know is the quiet beating of a heart which loves Him. Jesus should just hear "tick-a-tock, tick-a-tock," and he will know that every heartbeat is for him."

Richard did not consider this time of imprisonment wasted. He slept during the day and composed and delivered sermons each night. He even attempted to evangelize other inmates by tapping Morse code messages on the wall. He wrote, "Through this code you can preach the gospel to those who are to your right and left. The prisoners always change. Some are taken out from the cell and others are put in."

Two years later, Sabina was also arrested. She later described that moment:

We had to dress in front of six men. They trampled over our things. From time to time they shouted out, as if to encourage each other to keep up the meaningless search: "So you won't tell us where the arms are hidden! We'll tear this place apart!"

I said, "The only weapon we have in this house is here." I picked up the Bible from under their feet.

[One of the men] roared, "You're coming with us to make a full statement about those arms!"

I laid the Bible on the table and said, "Please allow us a few moments to pray. Then I'll go with you."

Sabina was taken to work on the Danube Canal (a project which was never completed). Mihai, their nine-year-old son, was left homeless. Sabina spent three years working at penal labor. During this time she was frequently interrogated by her captors. She recounted:

They shouted and bullied. Questions, questions. Some I couldn't answer. Some I wouldn't. It was a long session and I became confused by the noise and blinding light. My head whirled. They said, "We have methods of making you talk which you won't like. Don't try to be clever with us. It wastes our time. It wastes your life." The repetition and the insistence were maddening. My nerves were stretched to breaking point. It was hours before they sent me back to the cell.

Her cell offered little reprieve.

People learn what it means to be on this earth with nothing to do when they enter prison. Not to wash, or sew, or work. Women talked with longing about cooking and cleaning. How they would like to bake a cake for their children, then go round the house with a duster, and clean the windows, and scrub the tables. We had nothing even to look at. Time did not pass. It stood still.

Eventually Sabina was released, but she was greeted with the worst news imaginable. Secret police, posing as former prisoners, claimed to have attended Richard's funeral in prison. Her husband, she was told, was dead.

But this was not true. Richard was being moved from prison to prison – from Craiova to Gherla, Văcăreşti, Malmaison, Cluj, and Jilava. He experienced extreme physical torture during this time. The guards beat the soles of his feet until the skin tore off, then again until they exposed bone.

After eight and a half years in prison, Richard was discovered by a Christian doctor pretending to be a Communist Party member, and was finally released in a general amnesty in 1956. Strictly warned not to preach, he went immediately back to his work in the underground church.

In 1959 he was arrested again after an associate conspired against him. He was accused of preaching against communist doctrine, and sentenced to twenty-five years in prison. As he embraced his wife before leaving her for the second time, she encouraged him to keep up their evangelistic work, saying, "Richard, remember that it is written, 'You will be brought before rulers and kings to be a testimony unto them.'"

This time the psychological torture was even worse than physical pain. As Richard recorded it:

> We had to sit seventeen hours with nothing to lean on, and you were not allowed to close your eyes. For seventeen hours a day we had to hear, "Communism is good, Communism is good, Communism is good, etc.; Christianity is dead, Christianity is dead, Christianity is dead, etc.; Give up, give up, etc." You were bored after one minute of this but you had to hear it the whole seventeen hours for weeks, months, years even, without any interruption.

During Richard's second imprisonment, Sabina was once again told that her husband had died. This time she did not believe it. In 1964, due to increased political pressure from Western countries, Richard was once again granted amnesty and released. Fearing that he would continue getting himself arrested, the Norwegian Mission to the Jews and the Hebrew Christian Alliance negotiated with Romanian authorities to release Richard and Sabina from the country for $10,000. Although at first he refused to leave his home country, Richard was later convinced by fellow leaders of the underground church to become a voice in the West for the persecuted church.

In 1966 Richard testified before the US Senate's Internal Security Subcommittee. During his testimony, he pulled off his shirt to reveal eighteen deep scars from the torture he had experienced in the communist prisons. "My body represents Romania, my country, which has been tortured to a point that it can no longer weep," he told the subcommittee. "These marks on my body are my credentials."

In April 1967, Richard and Sabina formed an interdenominational organization to support the persecuted church in communist countries. They called it Jesus to the Communist World. But as they expanded their mission to include persecuted Christians in other parts of the world, including Muslim countries, the organization was renamed The Voice of the Martyrs. Because of his influential work, Richard became known as "The Voice of the Underground Church."

In 1990, after the collapse of the Soviet Union, the Wurmbrands finally returned to Romania. They had spent twenty-five years in exile from their homeland. The Voice of the Martyrs opened a printing facility and bookstore in Bucharest. The new mayor of the city offered a storage space for their books: under the palace of former dictator Nicolae Ceaușescu, where Richard had been held in solitary confinement for three years.

Though Richard retired from his work with The Voice of the Martyrs in 1992, he and Sabina continued to support the organization and the world's underground churches. Sabina died in 2000 and Richard in 2001.

27

Tulio Pedraza

persecuted from 1949 to 1964, in Colombia

WHEN MISSIONARIES ARRIVED in Colombia to establish the country's first Mennonite congregations, Tulio Pedraza and his wife Sofía became two of their first converts. They were baptized in June of 1949. Only a year earlier, Jorge Eliécer Gaitán, a liberal political candidate, had been assassinated; his death ignited a civil war that would last for ten years. Because Protestantism was seen as another threat to Colombia's already strained unity, Colombian Protestants faced significant opposition from municipal authorities, Catholic priests, and their own neighbors.

Tulio was a coffin maker in the small town of Anolaima. He was also blind. This didn't keep his business from becoming successful enough to provide for his family, since he was the only coffin maker in the town. But when the local Catholic priest learned about Tulio's baptism, he began making life difficult for the Pedraza family.

First he declared Tulio's "Protestant" coffins unfit for Catholics to be buried in. From the pulpit, he told parishioners that he would not officiate any funeral using a coffin purchased from the Mennonite. Business plummeted. Tulio could only sell coffins to close friends and those ignorant of the priest's declaration. And even those customers were forced to travel to surrounding towns to hold their funeral services, since the local priest refused to preside.

Then the priest took steps to ensure that even these trickling sales would end. He met a carpenter in another small town. The priest helped procure a house and tools for this carpenter and convinced him to move to Anolaima to begin a rival coffin business. After the arrival of this new competition, Tulio could no longer pay his suppliers. He was forced to close his business.

Though he was unsure of what to do next, Tulio never abandoned the love and decency he learned by imitating his Lord. Rather than begrudging the rival coffin maker, he reached out to him in friendship. When the blind man's own business collapsed, he sold this competitor his tools. Through this gesture of benevolence, he helped establish the business of the very man whose presence finished his.

Tulio and his wife did whatever they could to make ends meet. They tried to start a bakery, a chicken farm, and a candle-making business, but with little success. Tulio's expertise was in coffin making. None of these new businesses could bring in enough income to provide for the family. Tulio became more discouraged with every failed venture, but his faith gave him the strength to persist.

Their struggles were exacerbated by other acts of persecution. Writing shortly after Tulio lost his coffin business, local Mennonite missionary Gerald Stucky reported:

> The persecution has continued. Tulio's children were humiliated in the public school because they are Protestants. His property and

the lives of his family have been continually menaced. People who were his friends now refuse to speak to him on the street; stores refuse to sell to him; he has become an outcast for the cause of Christ. In spite of this, Tulio continues firm in the faith, trusting in the Lord day by day. He holds no evil in his heart towards those who have worked evil against him. He continues to witness to the light he found in Christ. Tulio is a living witness to the power of the gospel to overcome evil with good.

On more than one occasion, Tulio's life was threatened for religious reasons. After one particularly frightening encounter, he and his wife spent the night in the refuge of a Mennonite school in the nearby town of Cachipay.

Tulio died peacefully in 1964. The rival carpenter who had been brought in to destroy the Pedraza business donated a coffin for Tulio's burial. Even though the funeral was a Mennonite service, the coffin maker attended, risking his own reputation in the community to honor a man who had shown him such unusual love, born from a deep faith.

28

Stanimir Katanic

persecuted from 1950 to 1957, in Yugoslavia

WHEN STANIMIR KATANIC appeared before a Yugoslavian draft board on his twentieth birthday in 1950, he told the men sitting before him that he would do whatever tasks were required in military service as long as they did not compromise his faith. His position was clear: "I will swear no oath of allegiance to an earthly government and I refuse to use a weapon to kill another person."

At the time, every man in Yugoslavia was required to report for military service when he turned twenty. This conflicted with Stanimir's Nazarene faith. The Nazarenes, an Anabaptist movement with Slavic roots, were opposed to military service and all forms of violence. Stanimir knew his quiet defiance would provoke a harsh response, but he held to his convictions all the same.

The young man was sent before a military judge, who sentenced him to four years in prison. His hands were bound, and he was delivered to a prison in Foča. The guards issued him gray coveralls, assigned him to a room, and for the rest of his sentence called him only by his prison number: 2032B.

Stanimir found himself in a room that housed over two hundred prisoners. The few cots available to sleep on were assigned by seniority or claimed by bullies. The guards issued each prisoner two blankets. Stanimir slept on one and covered himself with the other. The prison floor was unbearably cold in winter and the air mercilessly hot in summer.

Stanimir didn't sleep much those first few nights, anyway. Many of the inmates who shared his space were convicted of violent crimes and had reputations for being dangerously unstable. The guards were known for violence as well. But while other prisoners were attacked by fellow inmates or beaten by guards, Stanimir stayed quiet and out of the way. He was largely ignored. There were other Nazarene consciencious objectors in the prison, but the guards kept them separate from each other so that they would not have the comfort of companionship.

In the mornings, the prisoners were taken to the yard. Their guards forced them to march in a circle for an hour – hands tied, eyes forward, no talking. Stanimir endured this punishing routine through torrential rain, sweltering heat, and frigid cold.

Stanimir and the other prisoners would then stand in two long lines: one for the morning portion of gruel, and the other for the day's ration of stale bread. In the gruel line, he would pull his bowl out from where he always kept it hidden in his vest, the server would ladle the slop in, and he would quickly tuck the bowl back into his vest when he was finished. He would hide his loaf under his two blankets for later in the day, but he rarely found it on his return.

During the day, Stanimir worked in the woodshop – head down, mouth shut – for long, dreary hours. At night he lined up for the scanty evening portion of gruel. Each day, he would wait anxiously to see if he had received a package from friends or family. Although they sent many, few were actually delivered. What letters he received he read over and over – they were his only reading material. He was not allowed a Bible.

Four long years passed. Finally, Stanimir's sentence was up. When he was released he returned home to marry Kata, a girl he'd known since childhood. Soon they were expecting their first child. His trials in prison had been brutal, but now his perseverance would be rewarded. Then, only ten months after his release, Stanimir received a letter demanding his appearance in court.

The judge asked, "Are you now ready to do what is right, and honorably defend your country?" Stanimir quietly replied, as he had the first time, that he could not swear allegiance to any government, nor could he kill another human being.

The ensuing sentence was even harsher than the first. The soon-to-be father was declared a political criminal. He was not even allowed to speak to his family. Hands tied, he was taken away to serve a new, four-and-a-half-year sentence in Goli Otok, a high-security prison located on a remote island in the Adriatic Sea.

His days were once again filled with heavy labor, extreme temperatures, violent inmates, and cruel guards. Days blurred into weeks, then months, then years. This windy island was a world away from his wife and the child he'd never met. Then, for unknown reasons, Stanimir was released a year early.

After three and a half years at Goli Otok, Stanimir Katanic was reunited with his wife. She introduced him to a young boy named Miroslav – his son.

In 2014, Stanimir, now an eighty-three-year-old man living in Ohio with his wife, Kata, recounted his story. He spoke in Serbian, and his son Miroslav translated. When asked, "On reflection upon all the years spent behind bars during the prime years of your life in harsh conditions, apart from your home and family and son, would you have done anything differently?" the old man replied, "I never look for shortcuts in my faith – and neither should you."

Reported by Marcia Lewandowski

29

Samuel Kakesa

persecuted 1964, in the Congo

WHEN SAMUEL KAKESA answered the knock at his door, he found a group of *jeunesse,* members of a young, rag-tag rebel militia, standing on the other side. "We understand that you have a shortwave radio in your home," they said.

"That is correct," Samuel answered.

"Well, our commander, Pierre Mulele, needs one at our bush headquarters, and he is sure you would be happy to donate it to the cause of the *jeunesse.*"

Samuel stood to the side. The rebels confiscated the shortwave radio – transmitter, battery, and antenna, which they retrieved from a nearby palm tree where it was strung.

Without the radio, Samuel, who lived with his wife and children in Mukedi, was cut off from the outside world and unable to do his job. The shortwave was his link to the other mission posts of his organization, the Congo Inland Mission (now the Africa Inter-Mennonite Mission). When the foreign missionaries who had established the Mennonite Church of Congo left the country, Samuel became the church's first Congolese legal representative. Among other responsibilities, he was the liaison between his church and the Congolese government. The government was subsidizing school programs and teachers' salaries, and it was up to Samuel to distribute this money to its intended recipients throughout Kwilu Province.

It was shortly after January 1964, when the *jeunesse* had overtaken Kwilu Province. Their leader, Mulele, was a Maoist revolutionary who had spent some time studying for the Catholic priesthood before turning to politics. He had served as the Congolese minister of education in the cabinet of Prime Minister Patrice Lumumba, but when Lumumba was assassinated in 1961, Mulele took up arms against the new regime. In 1963 he accompanied a group of young Congolese men to China for guerrilla warfare training. Maoist influence permeated Mulele's approach to warfare. He adapted Mao Zedong's writings to develop a code of conduct for rebel use:

1. Respect all men, even bad ones.

2. Buy the goods of villagers in all honesty and without stealing.

3. Return borrowed things in good time and without trouble.

4. Pay for things which you have broken and in good spirit.

5. Do not harm or hurt others.

6. Do not destroy or trample on other people's land.

7. Respect women and do not amuse yourselves with them as you would like to.

8. Do not make your prisoners of war suffer.

But, as Samuel Kakesa would learn, Mulele and his young forces, faced with the realities of guerrilla warfare, at times failed to hold to these well-intentioned ideals.

Samuel hoped he would not have any more unpleasant dealings with the rebels, but a few weeks later they returned. "Commander Mulele wants to meet you," they said. These were not men to say no to lightly. The fighters escorted Samuel back to their headquarters, a journey of several days. There they fed him, offered him a place to sleep, and told him that he would meet Mulele in the morning.

The next day he was taken before the rebel commander. "You are the legal representative of a large church?" Mulele asked. "Large sums of money pass through your hands for village teachers of your region?"

"That's correct," said Samuel.

Mulele frowned. "I've been receiving complaints from teachers accusing you of failing to deliver their salaries on time." He gestured toward a number of letters sitting on his desk.

Samuel tried to explain: "Since your men arrived in the area, all contact has been cut off with the church headquarters at Tshikapa. There is no way for them to transfer the funds to me, but I am sure the salaries are being held for the teachers."

The rebel commander leaned back in his chair and drummed his fingers. Finally he said, "For the time being, you are our prisoner. We'll talk again soon."

Samuel was taken to a small, dirt-floored cubicle made of sticks and thatch. The only furniture was a bench to be used as a bed. Through the slits in the walls, Samuel watched as rebels returned with goods they had stolen and captives to question. Anyone accused of opposing the *jeunesse* received harsh punishment. More than once, Samuel saw them kill a prisoner in the yard.

About a week passed, a week of watching and waiting. Then Samuel received a visitor – a friend from Mukedi. This friend passed along news from home and a change of clothes from Samuel's father.

After the visitor had left, Samuel discovered a small Gipende New Testament folded into the packet of clothing. This made his time in the cramped cell more bearable.

A few days later, Samuel was surprised to hear the familiar voices of his church colleagues. The rebels were using his stolen shortwave radio and had stumbled on the frequency used by the missionaries. *At last,* he thought, *I can prove my story.*

He called a guard over and asked to see Pierre Mulele. When the guards brought him before their commander, Samuel said, "If I can prove to you that all of the teachers' pay I've supposedly misused is in Tshikapa, will you believe me?"

Incredulous, Mulele asked, "You'll prove that to me how?"

Reception on the radio was spotty and Tshikapa missionaries were not always available, but Samuel decided to take a chance. "Tomorrow at noon," he said, "go with me over to that shed where you put the shortwave radio taken from my home, and I'll prove that I'm telling the truth."

The next day, they gathered at the allotted time. Mulele warned Samuel Kakesa not to use the radio to call for help. "If you say anything that would betray us or our cause, you will die on the spot." Samuel sat in the chair and brought the microphone to his lips. He used the call letters for Tshikapa. His heart pounded. Static.

Then a voice broke through: "Kakesa, is that you? Is that really you? I've been trying to contact you for weeks. Where have you been? Where are you now? We have urgent business with you. There is much accumulated mail for your area and we also have several months of salaries for the teachers that we need to get to you as soon as possible. Set a day and time when we can meet you at the Loange River, so we can bring all of this to you."

Glancing up at Mulele, Samuel answered, "I am well, but I'm not able to meet you now. I'm surrounded by soldiers. The matter of the mail and the money will have to wait." He turned the radio off, stood up, and asked Mulele, "Now do you believe me?"

The commander answered, "Yes, I now believe you. You are no longer a prisoner, but I cannot allow you to leave our camp. You are too valuable a person. You have much to offer our cause."

Samuel was taken to Mulele's office. He was commanded to transcribe the rebel leader's handwritten notes on a typewriter. Samuel was glad to have this new role to stay busy, but the contents of the notes troubled him. Among other things, he was typing out instructions to dig a trench in the middle of a road and to camouflage it, creating a deadly trap for passing vehicle convoys. He also transcribed instructions on the best way to burn down buildings made of permanent materials. One day he came across orders to coerce an unwilling village chief to be compliant.

Finally, Samuel could take it no longer. He thought to himself, *I'm contributing to the destruction of my own homeland and the suffering of my own people. I'm being used by this violent movement.* He could not oppose the rebels physically – he would certainly be killed, and more importantly, he was determined to practice nonviolence. So he decided to resist his captors in another way: by being unabashed about his faith. He knew the risk he was taking; Mulele's forces were targeting Western missionaries and their associates, and three Belgian Catholic priests had already been killed.

Every evening Samuel walked some distance from the rebel camp, sat on a log, and openly read the New Testament smuggled to him by his father. It wasn't long before the rebels reported what he was doing to Mulele. At that moment, Samuel could have ended his routine to preserve his safety, but he decided that he could not do so and still remain faithful to his Lord. He continued his evening ritual despite the great danger.

A few days later, the rebel commander approached Samuel as he read his New Testament. They looked at each other in silence for some time. Then, without saying anything, Mulele turned around and walked back to camp. Samuel turned back to his New Testament and continued praying.

When he returned to the camp later that evening, Samuel was sure the guards would take him out into the yard to punish him or even execute him, as he had seen them do to others many times before. He did not expect to see the next day. But the night came and went, and no one came to drag him out. Commander Mulele must have had decided to tolerate his activity.

One day while reading his Bible, Samuel thought he heard a voice saying, "Go to Mukedi." He didn't know it at the time, but believers in Mukedi had been praying that he would fall ill and be sent to their hospital for treatment. Shortly afterward his feet, hands, and legs began swelling – possibly a diabetic reaction to the starchy diet. Mulele gave him permission to go to Mukedi for treatment, accompanied by guards.

Meanwhile, back at home, Samuel's wife, Françoise, who was pregnant, began bleeding. She was rushed by Samuel's father on a bicycle to the Mukedi hospital. On the way she delivered twin girls. The first was born dead. She and her surviving newborn arrived at the hospital ahead of Samuel. When he unexpectedly appeared in her room, she hardly recognized him because his limbs were so swollen.

From the hospital, Samuel was able to escape into government-controlled territory, and shortly thereafter the rebellion was crushed. Samuel resumed his responsibilities and led efforts to establish the church in the region.

After his defeat, Mulele went into hiding in exile. Three years later he was promised amnesty by Congolese president Mobutu. But when the former guerilla leader returned to Kinshasa he was tried and executed, and his body was dumped in the Congo River.

Why, when the communist rebel Pierre Mulele had come upon Samuel Kakesa in prayer and Bible study, did he turn a blind eye to his prisoner's defiant expression of faith? Perhaps he recalled his own devotion earlier in life. Or he may have respected the prisoner's pluck. Or maybe his strict Maoist code of conduct stayed his hand. But Samuel had a different interpretation. Years later, when asked about the encounter, he replied, "It was the hand of God that restrained him. I stood between life and death during those moments. God still had more work for me to do."

30

Kasai Kapata

persecuted 1964, in the Congo

IN 1964, MAOIST REBELS under Pierre Mulele controlled most of Congo's Bandundu region. Many local Christians hid in the forests as Mulele's forces destroyed both Protestant and Catholic missions and sought to indoctrinate citizens with their brand of communism. Among the missions that Mulele's forces ransacked as they expanded their control were Mennonite Brethren locations at Matende and Lusemvu. It was only a matter of time until the rebels arrived in the Kafumba area, where Kasai Kapata served the local mission.

Kasai, the son of a shaman, was not new to the Kafumba mission – he had received his education there. He became a Christian early in life, and now served under pastor Djimbo Kabala as his secretary and assistant in the mission church. As the rebels approached, the missionaries fled to the cities of Kikwit and

Leopoldville (now Kinshasa), the nation's capital. Pastor Kabala, not wanting to travel far, hid with others in the forests. Kasai decided to take his family to their home village near Gungo, but when they arrived, they found that Mulele's forces had already occupied the village.

Kasai could no longer outrun the rebels, so he accepted a job providing them with food. Mulele's men knew he had been a leader at the mission, so they often made his labor especially difficult. Still, others suffered far worse, and Kasai made the best of his situation. Reflecting on this time in forced labor, Kasai later said, "It was hard for me, as a Christian, to watch the beatings and killings that were going on, but I did have the opportunity to witness to the rebels and help foster peace among the villagers themselves."

After several months, Kasai decided to return to the Kafumba mission to check on the church members still living there. Under the pretext of returning to gather some of his family's belongings, Kasai set out to visit his former home. When he neared the mission, a group of Mulele's rebels stopped him. Many knew him from his work at the mission church. Some had been in his Sunday school classes. One of the fighters handed him a hoe and told him to dig his own grave.

While Kasai worked, he heard the rebels arguing. Many wanted to kill the pastor. One offered to drive a truck over his head. But some of his former Sunday school students wanted to keep him alive. No consensus was reached, so when the grave was deep enough, they simply buried Kasai up to his neck until they came to a conclusion.

Over the next days and nights, Kasai remained buried in his own grave. He watched and waited for the rebels to return and kill him. He saw the experience as a test given to him by God. "Would I persevere and stay with my calling to be a pastor?" Kasai later said, "Or would this experience suddenly shatter the reality of God's clear call just a couple of years before?"

The answer was soon revealed to his captors, who noticed that his demeanor was not what they expected. Instead of becoming fearful, desperate, or despairing, Kasai became *cheerful*. As rebel feet passed around his head, he told the men, "It's a good thing that I am here in this grave."

His captors were confused. Had their prisoner gone mad? His former students knew better – he was filled with love for his enemies. Finally, after three days buried in the grave, his advocates convinced the other rebels to release him.

Once free, he continued on his journey to the mission. It had been looted and vandalized by Mulele's forces. He set about the task of rebuilding, meeting with local believers until the rebels were ousted by Congolese government troops. The soldiers used the mission as a base of operations as they drove the Mulele rebellion from Bandundu. When they, too, had left, Kasai led the effort to gather the congregation from the forests and surrounding cities where they had fled.

Kasai was later asked to serve as hospital chaplain for the government hospital at Pai-Kongila and as pastor of his local congregation. His efforts eventually led to the birth of ten congregations, composed of more than 2,300 members in total.

When asked how he survived the ordeal of being buried alive with such a cheerful attitude, Kasai said, "I have discovered that the Lord cleanses us through these experiences. During a time of persecution the church becomes stronger."

31

Meserete Kristos Church

persecuted from 1974 to 1992, in Ethiopia

TODAY THE WORLD'S LARGEST Anabaptist churches are not in Europe, where the movement started, nor in America, which saw much of its growth, but on the continent of Africa. In Ethiopia, the Meserete Kristos Church has over two hundred thousand baptized members in 591 congregations and 863 church planting centers spanning the large nation. "This past year alone, 17,345 people were baptized," longtime missionary Carl Hansen reported in 2012.

The church, though strong in numbers now, had humble beginnings in the country. While Christianity, mainly in its local Orthodox form, has an ancient history in Ethiopia, Meserete Kristos (Christ Is the Foundation) only traces its roots back to the mid-twentieth century. In 1945, Mennonite missionaries arrived in Ethiopia to bring relief after the harsh Italian occupation, which had lasted from 1936 to 1941. Not recognized as missionaries by the government, they focused exclusively on relief efforts, starting a hospital and bringing in much-needed supplies. In 1948 they were granted permission to conduct missionary work, including education and evangelism, and began immediately.

Three years later their efforts had paid off – ten men were ready to become the first group baptized by Mennonites in Ethiopia. There was just one problem. The men lived in the central town of Nazareth (renamed by Emperor Haile Selassie after the biblical village), which was part of a region officially closed to proselytization. Attempting to skirt the restriction, they traveled with the missionaries to the capital city of Addis Ababa, an "open" area. They were baptized and returned to Nazareth, where the local governor, angry at the evasion, scolded the missionaries. The date of this baptism – June 16, 1951 – is the day the Meserete Kristos Church counts as its true beginning.

In January 1959 church leaders met in Nazareth to begin discussing the transfer of authority from Western missionaries to Ethiopian leaders. It was a gradual process, but by 1965 Ethiopian members had assumed executive leadership positions, with the missionaries taking support roles.

The following years saw growth in unusual and unexpected ways. An English class taught by a Meserete Kristos missionary using the Gospel of John as the textbook led to the founding of "Heavenly Sunshine," a passionate and theologically charismatic church. When later communist persecution forced Heavenly Sunshine and related churches to join Meserete Kristos, they brought their distinct spiritual characteristics with them, including mass prayer, spiritual warfare, and speaking in tongues, making the culture of Meserete Kristos considerably more Pentecostal than many Anabaptist churches.

This time of open growth would not last forever, though. September 12, 1974 saw a coup overthrow Emperor Haile Selassie, ending a monarchy that had ruled Ethiopia for centuries and successfully resisted the European colonialism that had subjugated most of the African continent. The communist regime that replaced the monarchy brought considerable reforms, many of which benefitted a nation in the midst of economic upheaval, famine, and other major problems. But in keeping with its ideology, the new government also repressed religion and curtailed other civil liberties, promoting an atheistic Marxism and banning competing literature and expression.

Overnight, Meserete Kristos was forced to become an underground church. Church documents and worship and study materials needed to be kept hidden and carefully smuggled when moved. Church members, with the rest of the population, were made to attend courses intended to reeducate them through Marxist propaganda and discourage them from holding any counterrevolutionary gatherings or ideas.

By 1977 the oppression had become acute. A new law stated that no one under the age of thirty was allowed to attend church. Those who violated it were to be arrested. Young church members responded by dressing in "older" fashions to avoid notice. Acts of overt persecution gradually increased. Young troublemakers were encouraged to harass and physically attack Meserete Kristos members.

In 1978 Meserete Kristos members and students associated with a Bible academy in Nazareth were called to the town's *kebele* (local administrative office) for interrogation. The *kebele*, tasked with implementing Marxist indoctrination in the region, was against all religion. Hoping to co-opt the entire educational system for its purposes, it was intent on harassing the academy's students and staff. "They wanted to beat us and put us in prison," Alemayehu, the administrator of the academy, recalled years later. At points during the meetings, *kebele* leaders brandished their guns at the Christians, attempting to intimidate them.

Finally, the *kebele* demanded that the academy students take an oath denying their beliefs. This prompted more tense meetings with the school staff. After prolonged questioning, Alemayehu finally said, "You can't force our minds. We will obey anything that does not go against our religion. But if you go against our religion, we will not obey you. We obey God. Our minds are God's property."

"What we cannot settle around the table," the *kebele* leaders replied ominously, "we will settle with our guns."

"Your guns," the Christian teacher answered, "are to protect us, not to kill us. But we are ready and happy to die for our faith." The situation was diffused without violence, but students of the academy were detained, and the forced indoctrination and harassment continued.

Alemayehu remembers praying during this time, "God, is it really this hard to follow you? Have our forefathers had this kind of problem? God, shall I leave you? But where would I go? It's not my wish to leave you, but the situation is pressing." Then God spoke to his heart, "You can endure this and come through it to a better time. Just be patient." Peace entered his soul.

Church members in Nazareth were imprisoned. The *kebele,* desperate for shows of loyalty to the regime, demanded that the believers raise their hand, curse their enemies, and shout, "The revolution is above everything!" They refused, receiving beatings and arrests. Church leaders appealed for their suffering brothers and sisters, but their pleas to the *kebeles* of the country were largely ineffectual.

Nathan Hege, one of the first Mennonite missionaries to arrive in Ethiopia, later wrote of the widespread ridicule aimed at Christians as part of this persecution:

It was indeed a fearful time. The Western reader in a democratic society can hardly grasp the extent of the ridicule heaped on evangelical believers. Radio programs and newspaper articles constantly called them foreigners, CIA agents, anti-progressives, reactionary elements, even dogs. Their experiences were like those of the early Christians, as the apostle Paul said, "We have become the scum of the earth, the garbage of the world" (1 Cor. 4:13). Yet, like Paul, when believers were cursed, they blessed; when persecuted, they endured; when slandered, they answered kindly.

Finally, in 1982, government workers arrived at each of the church's buildings with a harsh directive. "This church shall be closed," they announced, "and it will be the property of the Ethiopian government." The government seized all of Meserete Kristos's offices, property, buildings, and bank accounts. Six key leaders of the church were arrested: Kelifa Ali, Kiros Bihon, Shamsudin Abdo, Negash Kebede, Abebe Gorfe, and Tilahun Beyene. They would be jailed in poor conditions and under constant fear of execution for over four years. Church gatherings, meetings, and proselytization were strictly forbidden.

Their leaders were jailed, their church buildings taken, their lifestyle mocked and reviled, their resources confiscated, but the Christians of Meserete Kristos were not crushed. They began holding services in private. To skirt a law forbidding gathering in groups of more than five people, the church spread themselves out to worship – in groups of five – in the houses of members. The number of groups far exceeded the number of trained pastors in the community, so meetings were led by laypeople. Under constant danger of raids by the police, members entered and left houses one at a time, coordinating their movements to avoid suspicion. Information was communicated to the scattered church by word of mouth.

The government's crackdown on the church, combined with the faithfulness of the believers, had an unexpected effect. The network of five-person groups meant that the church members, sharing intimately in their homes with close and trusted friends, flourished. There was no space for grandiose religiosity. And as their neighbors and friends outside the church grew increasingly disillusioned with the Marxist government and began searching for truth, church attendance grew. The Meserete Kristos Church may have officially ceased to exist, but it had never been more alive. The church grew from five thousand to thirty-four thousand members during ten years underground.

In 1992, the regime shifted to more democratic systems of governing the nation. After a decade of hiding and invisible growth, the Meserete Kristos Church was finally able to reemerge and take possession of some of its property that had been seized. Two years later, in 1994, Meserete Kristos Church Bible Institute, which would later become Meserete Kristos College, was founded. Its roots went deep into the underground years, when leaders such as Yeshitila Mengistu, Kedir Dolchume, Tadesse Negawo, Siyum Gebretsadik, and Shemelis Rega informally trained elders and evangelists operating in the church network. This ability to effectively train new leaders, learned under oppression, has allowed for the explosive growth, in numbers and witness, that the church has seen since.

The work of the church, in the complex cultural and social realities of Ethiopia, continues to thrive, grow, and adapt. Six basic commitments define the church's life and mission: witness, teaching, giving, compassion, prison ministry, and peacemaking. Today, Meserete Kristos models strategies for evangelism, education, social action, and church life that stand as examples for congregations worldwide. Much of this is the fruit of persecution that was intended to stifle and crush the church, but which in reality only scattered seeds full of life across Ethiopia.

32

Sarah Corson

persecuted 1980, in Sapecho, Bolivia

I T   W A S   M I D N I G H T, and the jungle lay quiet in the moonlight. Miles from any city, Sarah Corson was certainly not expecting visitors in the remote South American village where she was spending the summer. Yet as she stood on the porch and bent to pull up the blanket over her sleeping son, she heard a sudden thump. Startled, she saw that a soldier had slipped into the water barrel. Peering across the clearing, she saw many more soldiers advancing through the shadows toward her hut.

That summer, the American missionary organization SIFAT (Servants in Faith and Technology) had sent Sarah with a team of seventeen young people to this Bolivian village as part of an ongoing project to help the impoverished residents develop sustainable agricultural practices.

A military junta had recently co-opted the national election, and unrest had broken out in the rural areas. The junta suspected that the American missionaries were encouraging the resistance, and had decided it was time to eliminate them from the equation.

Sarah was terrified. Her heart was beating so fast she thought her blood vessels would burst. She knew she had a responsibility for the team members inside the house, but she couldn't even call out to them. She was paralyzed with fear.

She had only seconds to pray before the soldiers found her. "God, if I have to die," she prayed, "take care of my family. And God, please take away this fear. I don't want to die afraid. Please help me to die trusting you." She was suddenly aware of the presence of God. She was ready to die, and even thought that through their deaths her group might accomplish things that they had not been able to accomplish with their lives.

She bravely stepped up to the closest soldier and uttered words she would never have thought to say on her own. "Welcome, brother," she called out. "Come in. You do not need guns to visit us."

The soldier jumped, then blurted out, "Not me. I'm not the one. I'm just following orders. There's the commander over there, he's the one."

Sarah raised her voice and repeated, "You're all welcome. Everyone is welcome in our home."

The commander ran up to Sarah, shoved the muzzle of his rifle against her stomach, and pushed her through the doorway. Thirty soldiers rushed into the house and began pulling everything off the shelves and out of drawers, looking for guns. They were convinced that Sarah and her team had political motivations.

Sarah picked up a Spanish Bible and turned to the Sermon on the Mount. "We teach about Jesus Christ," she said, "God's Son, who came into this world to save us. He also taught us a better way than fighting. He taught us the way of love. Because of him, I can tell you that even though you kill me, I will die loving you, because God loves you. To follow him, I have to love you too."

"That's humanly impossible!" the commander of the troops burst out.

"That's true, sir," Sarah answered. "It isn't humanly possible, but with God's help it is possible."

"I don't believe it."

"You can prove it, sir. I know you came here to kill us. So just kill me slowly if you want to prove it. Cut me to pieces little by little, and you will see you cannot make me hate you. I will die praying for you, because God loves you and we love you too."

The soldiers rounded up the missionaries and many villagers and were about to haul everyone off in trucks. Suddenly the commander changed his mind and brusquely ordered the women back to their houses. He told Sarah that they would have been gang raped in the jungle camp and he wished to spare them that, but that if it were discovered that he had released them he would probably pay with his life. The men who had been captured were loaded into trucks and driven away. Before leaving, the soldier said, "I could have fought any amount of guns you might have had, but there is something here I cannot understand. I cannot fight it."

As Sunday approached, the villagers warned the missionaries not to hold a church service, since the military would assume any gathering had a political agenda. But on Saturday night, Sarah received an unexpected message from the commander who had raided the village: he wanted to attend church on Sunday, and said that if Sarah did not come to pick him up in her vehicle, he would walk the ten miles to be there anyway.

The request sounded suspicious. Sarah decided that only those who were ready to risk their lives should attend church on Sunday. She sent around a message: "We will have a service after all, but you are not obligated to come. In fact, you may lose your life by coming. No one knows what this soldier will do. Do not come when the church bell rings unless you are sure God wants you to come."

When Sunday morning came, the church was packed. Shaking in their boots, the villagers gathered. The commander and his deputy arrived fully armed and sat down in the congregation, their faces giving no indication whether their purpose in coming was friendly or hostile. It was customary for the congregation to greet visitors personally with a handshake and hug during a welcome song before the service. Although Sarah was going to waive all but the song, the congregation spontaneously took up greeting the two visitors with handshakes and hugs. The first one to do so said, as he hugged the commander, "Brother, we don't like what you have done to our village, but this is the house of God, and God loves you, so you are welcome here." The others followed his lead.

The commander was completely taken aback. He addressed the people: "Never have I dreamed that I could raid a town, come back, and have that town welcome me as a brother." Indicating Sarah, he said, "That woman told me Thursday night that Christians love their enemies, but I did not believe her then. You have proven it to me this morning. . . . I never believed there was a God before, but what I have just felt is so strong that I will never doubt the existence of God as long as I live."

Two weeks later, all the men who had been imprisoned were returned to the village. The commander's last words to Sarah would stay with her the rest of her life: "I have fought many battles and killed many people. It was nothing to me. It was just my job to exterminate them. But I never knew them personally. This is the first time I ever knew my enemy face to face. And I believe that if we knew each other, our guns would not be necessary."

33

Alexander Men

died 1990, in Semkhoz, Russia

ALEXANDER MEN was born in Moscow on January 22, 1935, to Jewish parents. His father, Volf, was a non-practicing Jew, though he was still sympathetic to the Jewish community. Alexander's mother, Elena, had been involved in the Russian Zionist movement as a young woman. She now met with the congregation of Serafim Batukov, a priest of the "Catacomb Church," an underground branch of the Russian Orthodox Church that refused to cooperate with the Soviet government. When Alexander was seven months old, Batukov baptized him and his mother. The two of them moved to Zagorsk to join Batukov's community of faith.

While Alexander was still young, his father was arrested by secret police and sent to a labor camp in the Ural Mountains. Batukov became a father figure to the young boy, nurturing him in the faith. When Alexander was seven, Batukov died. In his final words to Alexander's mother, the priest said, "Thanks to what you are enduring and to the serious way you are raising him, your Alik will someday be a great man." Afterward, the scientist and theologian Boris Vasilev, a fellow member of the church, took young Alexander under his wing.

When Alexander was thirteen, he strode up to the Moscow Theological Seminary, boldly knocked on the door, and asked to be admitted. Though he was rejected, the dean of students admired the young man's gusto and obvious intellect. The two began a lifelong friendship. Undeterred by his rejection, Alexander continued his studies. When he was fourteen, he began writing a volume on the life of Christ. This first draft would eventually become the first volume in his series on the history of world religion.

In 1955 he entered college in Moscow and later transferred to Irkustsk, where he studied biology. His roommate and fellow biology student was Gleb Yakunin, an atheist. Through long conversations, Alexander convinced Yakunin to rejoin the Russian Orthodox Church, in which he had been baptized as an infant. Yakunin would later become a priest and a defender of human rights in the Soviet Union. He would eventually spend time in prison for his outspoken beliefs.

Yakunin's conversion might have been Alexander's most significant achievement while at the school in Irkustsk. But it was costly. With graduation less than a year away, the school expelled Alexander, accusing him of being "a practicing church member." The young man wore this label as a badge of honor.

Returning to the path he had started as a thirteen-year-old boy, Alexander entered seminary at Zagorsk. In 1958 he married Natasha Grigorienko. Later that year he became a deacon. He graduated from Leningrad Theological Seminary in 1960 and was ordained a priest.

Alexander's ministry grew. His writing and preaching articulated a rich, intellectually compelling Christianity, eloquently dismantling the Soviet position that only atheism was validated by science. His books were circulated in samizdat (the underground press), attracting thousands of young men and women to the faith.

Perhaps it was due to his position as a prominent opponent of Soviet ideals, but Alexander's ministry attracted members of the Russian intelligentsia. Among those he baptized were songwriter Alexander Galich, cultural commentator Nadezhda Mandelstam (whose husband, the poet Osip Mandelstam, died in a Soviet labor camp), and writer Andrei Sinyavsky, who spent seven years in a Russian gulag. He also pastored film director Andrei Smirnov and literary critic Lev Annensky, and officiated the funerals of famous singers Vladimir Vysotsky and Viktor Shalamov.

Alexander's writings also caught the attention of less sympathetic government officials and the Orthodox hierarchy. Many Orthodox leaders frowned upon his emphasis on ecumenism. Some, steeped in anti-Semitic prejudice, could not look past his Jewish heritage. The church, seeking to limit his influence, sent him from Moscow to the small, secluded parish of Novaya Derevnya. In a slow-burning betrayal, other Orthodox priests began to speak against him to their congregations, to the press, and to the government. Noting his increasing isolation, Soviet authorities saw their opportunity to silence him.

The KGB secretly watched Alexander for six years. In 1985 and 1986, they harassed him with searches and seizures of his property. He met with members of the KGB several times every week. While they threatened to deport or imprison him unless he publically denounced his ministry, he endured their pressure with calm determination. Eventually, he admitted that, in the past, he "hadn't always behaved with proper caution and had made mistakes." The KGB twisted this into the denunciation they were looking for; Alexander only meant it as a basic confession that any Christian might make. Later, when asked how he had endured all this harassment, Alexander responded, "I'm a priest, I can talk to anybody. For me it's not difficult."

The late 1980s were a time of turbulent change for the Russian people. As perestroika was implemented, many Russians saw it as the end of oppression and the beginning of long-awaited freedom. Alexander was more cautious. He once told a group of young professionals:

> People see perestroika as a kind of panacea. "Ah! Here's the solution for everything!" But that's not the way it works. We are living with the consequences of a colossal historical pathology. Our church, our Russia, have been virtually destroyed, and the damage lives on – in people's souls, in the work ethic, in the family, and in the conscience.

The Russian Orthodox Church, long suppressed, was quickly becoming a symbol of nationalism under the government of Mikhail Gorbachev. Alexander's warnings about too-close affiliation with the new power structures proved insightful. Growth in Russian nationalism also brought a resurgence of anti-Semitism in the nation and church. Alexander, an Orthodox priest of Jewish heritage, was speaking out against chauvinism, anti-Semitism, and false patriotism. His popularity made conservative members of the Orthodox clergy uncomfortable. Many in his local congregation were also Christian Jews. In the village of Novaya Derevnya, Alexander's church was mocked as "the synagogue."

As religious restrictions were lifted, Alexander broadened his ministry. He booked as many as twenty public speaking engagements each month and began appearing regularly on radio and TV. In 1990 alone, he helped develop the Russian Bible Society, founded the Open Orthodox University, and started a journal, *The World of the Bible*. How did he find the time for these new initiatives while maintaining his regular pastoral duties? "I volunteer; God provides the time," he said. He told his brother that during this time of unprecedented freedom he felt like "an arrow finally sprung from the bow."

But old prejudices haunted Alexander's ministry. Zealots in the Orthodox Church, angered by his ecumenical spirit, spoke of Alexander as a "secret Catholic" or a "crypto-Jew" embedded in the church to cause disunity. He became a target of Pamyat (Memory), an extremist anti-Semitic organization of Russian nationalists. They blamed Russia's troubles over the previous century on the Jews. The symbol Pamyat chose for its movement was an axe.

In September 1990, Alexander was offered the position of rector at a Christian university in Moscow and invited to host a television show. He received menacing letters, threatening death should he accept either position. Protestors began showing up at his lectures. On one occasion, a group shouted, "Get out, you Yid! Don't tell us about our Christian religion!"

Alexander himself took these threats in stride, choosing to ignore some of the threatening letters, and reading others in public to sap them of their intended terror. Thinking there was safety in numbers, friends and congregants began accompanying him on his journeys or speaking engagements.

When a friend suggested it would be safest for Alexander to emigrate to the West, the priest responded, "Why? If God hasn't turned away from me, I must stay and serve him. And if he has turned away, where could I hide?"

The night of September 8, 1990, Alexander lectured in Moscow. At one point he said:

> Some ants build; some ants sow and later reap the crop; and some apes fight and have wars, although they are not as cruel as people are. But nothing in nature, except for man, ever tries to think of the meaning of life. Nothing climbs above its natural physical needs. No living creature, except for a human being, is able to take a risk, and even the risk of death, for the sake of truth. Thousands

of martyrs who have lived are a unique phenomenon in the history of our solar system.

The next morning, Alexander left his house in Semkhoz around 6:40 a.m., walking the wooded path to the local railway station. From there, he would ride by train twenty miles to his pinewood parish church. It was a routine he repeated every Sunday.

This morning was different, though. Only twenty minutes after he left, Alexander's wife, Natasha, awoke to the sound of groaning coming from outside the house. Looking out, she saw a crumpled body beyond the garden gate. She could tell that, whoever this person was, he was in need of assistance – probably drunk – so she called an ambulance. The man didn't move. A crowd was gathering. She opened the door and walked out. As she approached, the situation slowly dawned on her. As tears began to fall, she said to the crowd, "Don't tell me."

It was Alexander. Blood flowed from a four-inch wound in the back of his head. He was already dead.

The police examined the evidence at the site of the murder – a grove of trees within earshot of Alexander's house. Eventually they pieced a story together: "An unknown assassin jumped out of the woods at him and delivered the lethal blow," reported police officer Stepan Astachkov. "We found traces of blood and a struggle. The severely wounded man managed to stagger back to the gate of his house, where he fell." The attacker had chosen an unorthodox weapon for the assault: an axe.

Alexander's funeral, held in the courtyard of the church he had served, was a diverse gathering. Parishioners, friends, and family mingled with reporters and public figures whom Alexander had influenced during his ministry. Gleb Yakunin, Alexander's college roommate, gave the eulogy. He now served as a member of parliament, but no political risk would keep him from presiding over the funeral of his friend.

Alexander's death was widely covered by the Russian press. Even *Izvestia,* the government-sponsored paper, wrote, "He was the pastor to many human-rights champions, prisoners of conscience, those who were persecuted by the authorities. His work in providing spiritual support to many intellectuals in disgrace brought him true friends, but also real foes." President Mikhail Gorbachev demanded a thorough investigation into the killing, and the Orthodox Church commissioned its own investigation.

Several people were detained, but no one was ever charged. The police eventually said that the most likely motive for the killing was robbery, since Alexander's briefcase was missing after the attack and the forest path had a history of crime. Those close to Alexander continued to believe the murder was a planned assassination; they remembered the threatening letters he had received in the months before his death. Some claimed he was at the top of a hit list of enemies that had been created by Pamyat. Others suspected his earlier confrontations with the KGB had something to do with the attack.

Whatever the true circumstances, Alexander's murder was the culminating moment in a long line of persecutions throughout his ministry. These personal attacks never deterred him from following Jesus, whom he had loved since his boyhood. He always believed that God's goodness would triumph over evil. One reporter noted that the closing words of Alexander's last article could have been his epitaph. He had written: "Chaos growing out of tyranny will not endure. No matter how long the darkness, the night cannot be endless. God's word teaches us to believe in the victory of the light."

Adapted from an account by Larry Woiwode

34

José Chuquín
and Norman Tattersall

died 1991, in Lima, Peru

MAY 17, 1991 marked the eleventh anniversary of the founding of Sendero Luminoso (Shining Path), a communist guerrilla group known for its fierce opposition to outside influence in Peru. Its war with the government had already claimed tens of thousands of lives in the impoverished South American nation.

That day, two foreign aid workers employed by the relief organization World Vision drove through Lima, the nation's capital. Norman Tattersall, a Canadian who had grown up as a son of missionaries in Colombia, was acting director of World Vision Peru. He had been working in Peru for over a year, running relief efforts in Lima and surrounding cities, including the rebel-controlled stronghold of Ayacucho. A significant portion of his time was spent fighting Peru's cholera epidemic.

Norman's companion, José Chuquín, was president of the Colombian Mennonite Church, and for the past eleven years, the director of World Vision's operations across the border in his native Colombia, where he oversaw seven hundred employees and volunteers. He was currently working with Norman to extend their efforts into Peru. José had been born in La Florida, Colombia, in 1946. He grew up on a small coffee farm, attended the Mennonite school in Cachipay, Colombia, and eventually went to college in North Carolina. He met and married Laura Broad there in 1976. They had five children.

José's work flowed from his strong personal faith. He worked to deliver emergency aid to the needy, but also to improve their lives and communities. He said he was committed "not only to the Mennonite Church where I am a member, but to the church as a whole, and especially to those Christian brothers and sisters who are eager to learn more about holistic social development."

As leaders of a foreign-funded Christian aid organization, Norman and José were prime targets for the Shining Path, whose members believed foreign aid workers and missionaries undermined their efforts to establish a "pure" communism. World Vision staff had received repeated death threats labeling the organization "an opiate of the people," as Karl Marx had once famously denigrated religion. Shining Path had issued a demand that the organization leave Peru. Despite these threats, however, the work continued.

The two men and their driver, staff member José Zirena, were driving through the city toward the World Vision office. It was a quiet Friday morning; the two were scheduled to leave Lima that weekend. As they arrived at their headquarters, two men pulled up alongside them. There was a deafening blast of automatic gunfire as the attackers emptied their weapons into the vehicle. Dozens of rounds of ammunition perforated the car, puncturing metal, ripping seats, and shattering glass.

11

The driver somehow escaped injury in the hail of bullets. His passengers did not. Norman died immediately, riddled with twenty bullet wounds throughout his head and upper body. José was critically wounded, taking at least twenty-two bullets, mostly to his lower torso and legs.

José was rushed to the nearest hospital, and then flown to Norfolk, Virginia, where he underwent seven hours of surgery. His colleagues and family prayed fervently for him as he fought for life. They also prayed for his attackers. He was reported to be improving, but the improvement was only temporary. His wounds became infected and he died on May 28, eleven days after the attack. His body was returned to Colombia for burial.

A professional investigation failed to turn up any leads on who the killers might be or to confirm the motive behind the attack. No person or group claimed responsibility for the murders, though circumstantial evidence strongly suggests Shining Path's involvement.

Graeme Irvine, former president of World Vision Australia, wrote of José's death, "For most of us, even those who travel to dangerous places, this kind of violence seems to belong only in movies and novels. But in reality, evil always lurks in the shadows, especially where the servants of Jesus Christ work for change and justice among the poor."

Dr. Valdir Steuernagel, a Brazilian member of the organization's international board, wrote, "This is a painful hour. . . . It is very hard that the impoverishment experienced by most of our societies in Latin American also embodies a process where life becomes very cheap. How to rescue the sanctity of life in the midst of a society in decomposition is quite a challenge. But it must be faced in the name of Jesus."

Because of the attack and other violence against their staff and other foreign workers, World Vision pulled out of Peru at the end of 1991, with the exception of a small staff remaining in Lima.

This ended crucial support to some twenty-three thousand households in impoverished communities throughout the nation. But the setback was not permanent. Today World Vision's mission, for which José Chuquín and Norman Tattersall gave their lives, is active again in Peru, with over eighteen thousand children receiving aid and education.

35

Katherine Wu

persecuted 1993, in Taiwan

IN 1986, KATHERINE WU, a Mennonite in Hualien, Taiwan, established the Good Shepherd Center to minister to girls rescued from prostitution. Katherine conceived of the center as a place for these abused girls to be educated and learn new skills to help them seek a better vocation and life.

The center was a peaceful response to a terrible crisis. According to child advocacy groups, sixty thousand children in the country worked as prostitutes at the time. When aboriginal Taiwanese families on the island's east coast encountered desperate financial troubles, many would sell their daughters into the sex trade. The organized criminals running this shadowy "industry" didn't appreciate people like Katherine hurting their "business."

One morning in 1993, Katherine arrived at work as usual, preparing for the day's tasks at the center. Three hooded figures appeared behind her and seized her. "When they first grabbed me, I thought it was a robbery," Katherine wrote in a report on the incident. "When they stuffed rags into my mouth, I thought that someone wanted to kidnap me to get something from my husband. When they started to punch me, I knew that it was because of my work at Good Shepherd."

The three attackers beat Katherine until she was nearly unconscious. With the last of her strength, she reached out and rang the doorbell. Staff members came to the door and the attackers ran off. The staff rushed Katherine to the hospital.

While Katherine recovered, friends, family, and Good Shepherd staff came to visit her. They all repeated the same advice: she should leave her work at the center to save herself. "The next time they will kill you," they said. Katherine answered them bravely, "Jesus loves those girls, and I love them too." Her recovery took several weeks.

As soon as she could, Katherine returned to her work. But the threat of another attack hovered over everything she did. "When I walk outdoors, I am always looking behind me to see if anyone is following me," she told someone not long after the attack. How could she continue working under such stress? In an interview, she attributed her perseverance to reading God's Word and praying "moment by moment."

The national media picked up Katherine's story. It wasn't long before organizations, private individuals, and even the Taiwanese government were sending aid to fund Katherine and the Good Shepherd Center. Thanks in part to the widespread publicity around Katherine's story, the government passed laws to ban the sex trade and protect aboriginal children. But Katherine didn't take this victory as an excuse to relax her efforts. With her characteristic commitment to the vulnerable, she expanded the center from an outreach to former prostitutes into a ministry for all abused women.

36

Ekklesiyar Yan'uwa a Nigeria

persecuted from 2009 to the present, in Nigeria

IN 2009, Boko Haram militants entered Monica Dna's home in the middle of the night. Before Monica's eyes, they beheaded her husband and slit the throats of two of her three sons. Then, turning to her, they slashed her left arm as she raised it in defense, cut her throat, and left her for dead.

A neighbor found her still alive and took her to the hospital. Six years later, after numerous operations, she still needed more surgery. But dealing with the trauma of the attack and the loss of her husband and sons was even harder than recovering physically. She managed to endure only because of the strength she received from Jesus, and through the support of other displaced widows in Jos, the town in central Nigeria where she found refuge.

Monica was one of more than 1.5 million people displaced by violence in areas of northeastern Nigeria subject to attacks by the

Islamist organization Boko Haram. The group was first formed in 2002 to oppose government security forces and Western influence – *boko haram* is often translated as "Western education is forbidden." In March 2015, the group's leader, Abubakar Shekau, formally pledged allegiance to the Islamic State in Iraq and Syria (ISIS), and changed the group's official name to Wilāyat Gharb Ifrīqīyyah (West African Province) of the Islamic State. At the time, around twenty thousand square miles of territory were under its control.

When the militants started appearing in villages, residents later recalled, they would claim to be looking for a mosque to pray in. Soon after, they started giving out money to help Muslims develop their businesses; many took this money without understanding Boko Haram's goals. Next, they attacked a few churches and individual Christians. With time, they unveiled their plan of overthrowing the government and creating an Islamic state. In 2009 they launched a campaign of assassinations, bombings, and abductions targeting both Christians and non-cooperating Muslims.

In April 2014, Boko Haram gained the world's attention when it abducted 276 girls from their school in the town of Chibok. Of the abducted girls, 178 belonged to Ekklesiyar Yan'uwa a Nigeria (EYN), the Church of the Brethren in Nigeria. Founded by American missionaries in 1923, EYN eventually grew to become the largest Christian denomination in northeastern Nigeria. EYN belongs to the Anabaptist family of churches, tracing its roots to the sixteenth-century Radical Reformation. A fundamental tenet of Anabaptism for almost five centuries has been Christian nonresistance – a conviction for which Anabaptist churches have often paid dearly.

Now Nigerian Anabaptists, shaped by this heritage of nonviolence and martyrdom, found themselves carrying it forward. In fact, from 2013 to 2015 alone, more than three times as many Anabaptist Christians died at the hands of Boko Haram than were killed in all the persecutions of sixteenth-century Europe. By the summer of 2015, over ten thousand EYN members had been killed, and more than 170,000 members, including 2,092 pastors and evangelists, had been displaced within Nigeria or in neighboring countries. Boko Haram had destroyed 278 church buildings and 1,674 preaching points. Of the denomination's fifty church districts, only seven were functioning. In October 2014, militants destroyed EYN's national headquarters in Mubi, Adamawa, so the church set up temporary headquarters in the relative safety of Jos, where many displaced members had gathered.

Other Christians in Nigeria responded to Boko Haram's violence by taking up arms against the group; some congregations even formed militias. By contrast, EYN members largely remained true to their nonviolent convictions. As their stories attest, this faithfulness despite persecution allowed them to witness to Christ's way of peace and forgiveness, even toward their enemies.

Displaced families and individuals started coming in large numbers to Jos and other safer areas of Nigeria in the spring of 2014. When possible, they went to live with relatives. Still, thousands of once self-reliant people ended up in displacement camps; others camped outside on the grounds of church buildings. The EYN bought land near Jos and Abuja, the national capital, in order to build temporary housing. In the meantime, many EYN families opened their doors to the traumatized newcomers.

One such family, Janata and Markus Gamache, took in up to fifty-two displaced people at a time. At night their living room was filled with women and young children sleeping on mats, while the older children slept in the fenced-in yard and the men camped out under the trees. Most of the cooking was done in the back yard over a wood fire, in large pots resting on stones. Guests helped with cooking, shopping, buying firewood, cleaning, household repairs, and working in the family's poultry business. Janata organized everyone and saw to it that all the chores got done.

"Of course the work has increased," she said, weariness showing in her eyes. "We have to sanitize the rug and other parts of the house often to prevent illness. Buying all the food and supplies at an economical price, having seventeen children here, and sharing one bathroom are all challenging. When it gets too noisy in the evenings, I go outside, just to have a time of quiet."

Janata was hopeful that, with some of the areas in the Northeast becoming more stable, her household would gradually shrink in numbers as some returned home. "We have not been able to close our hearts to those in need," she said. "It's our Nigerian custom, but more importantly, it's what God asks of us: to care for people who have lost their homes and family and have nothing. And God is our main source of strength."

For Musa Ishaku Indawa, an EYN member living as a displaced person in Yola, the troubles started in November 2013. That's when Boko Haram attacked Ngoshe, his hometown, damaging churches, burning houses, looting, and stealing cars. They also killed Musa's uncle and four other church members. "Everyone was living in fear," Musa recalled later. "Some stayed in town, while others stayed out in the bush. But before the attacks, Christians in my home area [75 percent of the population] had been living in peace with our Muslim neighbors."

Five months later, in April 2014, Boko Haram militants returned and besieged the town, driving out the Nigerian military. Musa recounted:

From 7:30 that evening until 2:00 in the morning, there was no let-up of shooting. I was worried for my wife, who had given birth just weeks before, but I decided we had to leave. I held our baby to my chest, bent down, and we ran, trusting our safety to God. We saw only one militant as we fled to the mountains. Many others ran too.

When some time had passed, they went back home.

> But during a church meeting in early June, we heard shooting, and everyone ran to the mountains again. Boko Haram looted and burned more houses and churches; more church members were killed. The militants also surrounded the mountains, killing more than a hundred men and abducting women and children. Eventually, our family was able to leave and go south to Mubi, where I rented a farm and started farming. Then, after Boko Haram seized the nearby town of Michika, we left Mubi and traveled farther south, to Yola. After nine months in the mountains, my mother came out, and we found out that my father was dead. Now my mother is in Yola with us. Yet even now, people are still hiding in the mountains; some have died of hunger.

"We can't live for Christ without going through difficulties," Musa added. "Throughout this time, I continually prayed and trusted that if God wanted us to survive, he would protect us and give us the strength."

Like Musa, Rifkaty Bitrus and her family fled to the mountains when Boko Haram attacked Ngoshe. But in her case, the escape failed. The militants pursued them and abducted Rifkaty and her two daughters, ages one and four, along with many other women and girls.

At the Boko Haram camp, they were kept in a locked and guarded house. They were not harmed, but were forced to do jobs such as pounding palm oil and fetching water, with the gate locked behind them when they returned. "They called us unbelievers," she said, "and threatened to slaughter us like cows if we didn't convert to Islam. We had to wear the Muslim veil, but none of us converted."

After three weeks, Rifkaty managed to escape at night without the guard noticing. She helped her four-year-old daughter over the wall, then climbed over it herself with her baby on her back. With fifteen other women, they hid in the mountains and made their way over the border to Cameroon. There she reunited with her husband, and together they relocated to a camp near Jos. Rifkaty, while grateful to be alive, still did not know if her family members who stayed in Ngoshe had survived.

Some EYN members risked their lives to save their neighbors. In February 2014, Ibrahim Dauda knew he had to do something to help his neighbor, a woman who was bleeding severely after her unborn child had died. In spite of the dangers from nearby Boko Haram forces, he took her across the border to a hospital in Cameroon. Because he didn't have enough money for the operation that she needed, he gave the doctor what he had and, leaving his identification papers and church membership card at the hospital, told them that he would return with the rest of the money.

Six Boko Haram militants stopped him at the border. Ibrahim explained that he needed to go home to get the money for the woman's surgery. They let him go. Expecting them to ambush him when he returned with the money, he came back by a different road. He paid the hospital, and the woman lived.

Faced with such intense persecution, not all church members were able to hold fast to their convictions. Some, when threatened by Boko Haram, or having witnessed the torture or murder of family members, chose to abandon their church's teachings and used weapons in self-defense or retaliation. Others joined denominations that had formed Christian militias. Some even sought to save themselves and their families by converting to Islam. But such cases were exceptions; most EYN members and churches remained true to their peace heritage.

Adamu Bello, pastor of an EYN church in Maiduguri, the state capital of Borno, was visited several times by small groups of men who introduced themselves as Boko Haram militants – possibly to test him, or possibly to kill him.

"Because I was raised Muslim," he later said, "I know how they think and how to calm them down and make peace. I always spoke with respect, treating them as fellow human beings, trying to understand them." Each time, he asked about their problems and prayed with them. When they left, he sent a church member to accompany them out a back way so the Nigerian military wouldn't kill them. "I do this because I love you," he told them.

One day, he spoke with the man who washed his car about his concerns for the young men in Boko Haram. "When the Nigerian military finds them, it kills them right away," he told him, "but if I were a political leader I would pardon them if they would agree to stop fighting. I wouldn't kill any who were captured, but would have them brought to me. I would listen to them, try to understand, and do something about the problems they're angry about." At the time, he didn't realize that he was talking to a Boko Haram commandant.

Some time later, while driving with his family, he was stopped and surrounded by a large Boko Haram contingent. Bello expected to be killed, but one militant looked into the car window and recognized him. "He's a good man," he told the others. To Bello, he said, "You may pass." The family drove on without incident.

At an EYN workshop for trauma healing and reconciliation, Ibrahim Dauda, the man who faced down Boko Haram in order to help his sick neighbor, told the other participants:

> I know the people who stole my cows, goats, generator, motorcycle, and things in my house. When I came to my first trauma healing workshop, I was bitter and not ready to forgive Boko Haram. I

believed that justice should be done before I could consider forgiveness. Now I can forgive. I even called Boko Haram members and told them that I have forgiven them. They were surprised; some of them thanked me. When you forgive, you have new freedom.

"It's not easy," added Gabriel Vanco, from Uba. "All my life's work – my poultry farm, twenty-one cows, my harvested crops – was stolen. It's hard to go home and see your clothes being worn by one of your neighbors or your furniture in his house, but we must forgive to be free of the burden of hatred. And it's only by the grace of God that we can do it."

Reconciliation, they knew, would be needed if communities in Nigeria's Northeast ever hoped to rebuild. While episodes of violence between Muslims and Christians weren't unprecedented in the region, before Boko Haram the two faiths had mostly coexisted peacefully. Now many survivors were understandably bitter. "None of our Muslim friends helped us during the attacks," said one woman, standing at the site of a burned-out church building near Mubi, the town where dozens died in Islamist attacks in 2012. "Some helped Boko Haram carry them out. Now there's no trust between Muslims and Christians here."

Other survivors had more hopeful stories to tell. When Shawulu T. Zhigila, an EYN pastor, was hiding from Boko Haram forces in Ngoshe, Muslim neighbors took him into their homes to hide and protect him. They continued to call him occasionally after that, saying they were glad he was still alive.

Such acts of compassion go both ways, according to James Musa, another EYN pastor. "When we give out material aid and services, we give it to EYN members, but when possible also to others – Christian or Muslim – from the area who need it. They're all experiencing the same problems." He recounted how EYN members in Madagali, Adamawa, gave support and medicine to a sick Muslim woman who had been abandoned by her family when

Boko Haram attacked the town. She told them, "From now on I will be a Christian."

In May 2015, the Gurku Interfaith IDP Camp, a project initiated by Markus Gamache and other EYN members, officially opened with a joyful celebration. All of the 162 Muslim and Christian families who moved in had lost homes and livelihoods in the violence. Now they were settling into new three-room houses that they had helped to build from handmade mud bricks. Each family would farm on a plot of land while helping to build a school and clinic. Representing many tribes and languages, they would live together as a model for positive relationships between Christians and Muslims.

For some members of EYN, the work of reconciliation didn't stop with making peace with their Muslim neighbors. They sought to reach the hearts of the Boko Haram fighters themselves. In November 2013, Dr. Rebecca Dali, an EYN member who coordinates a relief organization, was delivering supplies in the Gawar Refugee Camp in Cameroon. A man whom she suspected to be a Boko Haram militant asked her to meet with him in private, saying, "I want to talk with you because you have the spirit of love." Rebecca later recalled:

> He admitted to being a Boko Haram fighter who had killed more than thirty-two people. I asked him to give that up and follow Jesus. As I prayed for him, he wept and accepted Christ as his Lord and Savior. He said that he would need to do this secretly at first, since his life would be in danger, but in time he would be able to practice his faith publicly. I connected him with one of the EYN pastors in the camp.

Another time, Rebecca was on her way to Chibok to deliver relief supplies when two militants stopped her car and forced her to follow them into the bush. Walking after them, she agonized, imagining her imminent death. She silently prayed, "God, if you want me to die, I will accept it, but if you want me to keep doing this work, protect me and let me live."

Twenty militants surrounded her, and one told her, "OK, we're going to kill you. Aren't you scared?"

"No," she answered. "I'm not scared. Even if I die, I know where I am going – to heaven."

"Where are the Boko Haram going," he asked her in return, "to heaven, or to hell?"

"I don't know, but I'm praying for you to go the right way. You always have a second chance. In one second, you can change your life and go to heaven."

He responded, "You're a good person. We will not touch you." Acknowledging that she was giving food and supplies to Muslims, he added, "Go and do your work!" As she left, Rebecca told them she would pray for them.

"The people desperately need help, so I will continue this work despite the danger," Rebecca said later. "God saved my life, and so the rest of my life is a bonus. And now they know that I distribute aid to Christians, Muslims, and pagans, and even have a Muslim on my staff, so they let me pass. When they came to Mubi and attacked, they damaged the EYN headquarters. But they didn't touch the warehouse with relief supplies."

Many church members say their faith was refounded and strengthened through this ordeal. One young man, a relative of Markus Gamache, said, "When I was captured by Boko Haram and forced to join them, I received 250,000 naira, a gun, and ammunition. We were all expected to kill one or two of our blood brothers. If you refused, they would kill you and take back what they had given you."

For a while, the young man said, he managed to avoid taking part in the raiding, looting, or killing by making an excuse to leave for family emergencies. But he knew he couldn't keep it up much longer. "I also didn't swallow the 'charm,' the drug they give you that makes you compliant and unable to think for yourself."

Before his capture, he had strayed from his Christian faith, but because he knew that what Boko Haram wanted him to do was evil, he returned to his beliefs. In captivity, he and several other Christians secretly communicated about how to escape. Finally he managed to escape into the bush and to contact Markus.

"Often Christians who have been with Boko Haram but have escaped are not accepted back into the Christian community," Markus explained, "but the people in the EYN congregation here have accepted him. And now his faith and determination to live it out have been strengthened by what he went through."

Like this young man, the church as a whole was strengthened through the hardships it encountered. At EYN's annual conference in 2015, Rev. Samuel Dali gave voice to the experience of the church: "We have been badly wounded. At first we felt confused, frustrated, and uncertain about the future, but we have never ceased to operate. We have made some painful progress, and we are recovering and gaining strength."

Such words of hope could not erase the horrors the church had experienced or the difficulties ahead. Many EYN members were still vulnerable, and displaced members often felt disconnected from the church. Those returning to their home communities would face the tremendous challenge of rebuilding and coping with trauma and wounded relationships. In Bible studies and sermons, EYN members often spoke of the persecution faced by the early Christians. They adopted Philippians 1:21 as their theme for the year: "For to me, to live is Christ and to die is gain."

Yet despite the challenges, many members of EYN said that the crisis had intensified their love and care for each other. And paradoxically, the scattering of the EYN church had spread its witness into new areas of Nigeria and even into neighboring countries.

"Faithful Christians should not fear death, but have hope, and follow God's leading to serve," Reverend Dali told the EYN staff. "We are to follow Christ, whether Boko Haram is threatening or not. If we live for Christ, Boko Haram has no power over us."

Written by Peggy Gish

Questions for Reflection and Discussion

These stories are meant to be shared. After you have read one or more with your family, congregation, class, or discussion group, use some or all of these questions to spark conversation and help apply these stories to our lives today.

1. What do you think makes someone a Christian martyr?

2. What points of faith are you personally willing to suffer and die for? What is non-negotiable for you?

3. If you were called to give an account of your faith, would you be ready and able to do so? If not, why not?

4. In many of these stories, Christians suffered on account of their boldness. What would happen if you were to become bolder about your faith? What hinders you from being more daring and outspoken?

5. Many of these stories show how Christ gives his followers strength to face opposition. Have you ever experienced this?

6. Tertullian once said, "The blood of the martyrs is the seed of the church." How does God use persecution to spread the gospel?

7. If the church is most vibrant under trial and tribulation, why do we seek a life free of danger?

8. How important is it for Christians to remain nonviolent in their witness?

9. Should a Christian ever actively resist the state? If so, when and to what degree?

10. Is working for justice and suffering as a result the same as bearing witness to the gospel? Does this distinction matter?

11. Do you think Christians, including those in North America and Europe, are facing increasing animosity? If so, why might that be?

12. In the past, many martyrs suffered at the hands of religious authorities. Can you see this happening again?

13. In the New Testament we read how the early Christians stood with those who were persecuted. How might we do this more faithfully today?

14. How have these stories affected you?

Notes on Sources

Introduction: Portions of the introduction, in a quite different form, appeared in "The Complex Legacy of the Martyrs Mirror," by John D. Roth, *The Mennonite Quarterly Review,* 87 (July 2013), 277–316.

1. **Stephen:** Abridged from *Acts of the Apostles,* Chapters 2–7. Direct quotes taken from the Holy Bible, New International Version, copyright ©1973, 1978, 1984, 2011 by Biblica, Inc. Used by permission. All rights reserved worldwide.

2. **Polycarp:** Taken from three different sources: "The Martyrdom of Polycarp" in *The Ante-Nicene Fathers,* edited by Philip Schaff, et al., translated by Marcus Dods (Peabody, MA: Hendrickson Publishers, 1996) is the most complete account. *History of the Church* in *Nicene and Post-Nicene Fathers, Series 2: Eusebius,* edited by Philip Schaff, et al. (Grand Rapids, MI: Wm. B. Eerdmans, 1984) includes valuable commentary by Eusebius. Finally, Irenaeus, *Against Heresies,* translated by Philip Schaff; edited by Alexander Roberts, et al. (Grand Rapids, MI: Wm. B. Eerdmans, 2001) contains details on Polycarp's earlier life and character.

3. **Justin Martyr:** Drawn primarily from Philip Schaff's collection on Justin Martyr in *The Ante-Nicene Fathers.* Schaff's introduction and textual notes give more detail to the story than is included here.

4. **Agathonica, Papylus, and Carpus:** Based on "Martyrdom of Carpus, Papylus, and Agathonicê" (third century) in *The Acts of the Christian Martyrs,* translated from the Latin by Herbert Musurillo (Oxford: Oxford University Press, 1972). An even earlier, and likely more reliable, Greek source reports that Agathonica was not sentenced to death but simply threw herself upon the pyre of the other two martyrs.

5. **Perpetua:** Based entirely on "Acts of Perpetua and Felicitas" in *The Ante-Nicene Fathers.* Most scholars agree that Tertullian authored the work, using the prison diaries and letters of Perpetua and Sarturus as resources, around AD 230.

6. **Tharacus, Probus, Andronicus:** Based on the account in *Martyrs Mirror of the Defenseless Christians,* by Thieleman J. van Braght, translated by Joseph Sohm (Scottdale, PA: Herald Press, 1938).

7. **Marcellus:** Based on a biography of Marcellus published in *In Communion* 47 (Fall 2007), a publication of the Orthodox Peace Fellowship. Additional quotes and information were drawn from *The Apostolic Tradition of Hippolytus,* translated by Burton S. Easton (Cambridge: Cambridge University Press, 1934).

8. **Jan Hus:** Based on articles by Elesha Coffman, Thomas A. Fudge, and Maartje M. Abbenhuis in *Christian History and Biography* 68 (October 2000).

9. **Michael and Margaretha Sattler:** Primarily based on *Anabaptist Portraits,* by John Allen Moore (Scottdale, PA: Herald Press, 1984). The account in *Martyrs Mirror* gave valuable additional details about Sattler's trial. Other details came from *The Radical Reformation,* by George H. Williams (Philadelphia: Westminster Press, 1962).

10. **Weynken Claes:** Based entirely on the account in *Martyrs Mirror.*

11. **William Tyndale:** Based on several sources, including the account in *Foxe's Book of Martyrs,* by John Foxe, edited by William Byron Forbush (Grand Rapids, MI: Zondervan, 1967); *Martyrs Mirror,* by van Braght; *God's Bestseller,* by Brian Moynahan (New York: St. Martin's Press, 2002); *Tyndale: The Man Who Gave God an English Voice,* by David Teems (Nashville, TN: Thomas Nelson, 2012); and *Christian History and Biography* 16 (October 1987).

12. **Jakob and Katharina Hutter:** Based on the account in *The Chronicle of the Hutterian Brethren,* vol. 1 (Rifton, NY: Plough, 1987) and Johann Loserth's entry on Jakob Hutter in the Global Anabaptist Mennonite Encyclopedia. See also Werner O. Packull, *Hutterite Beginnings: Communitarian Experiments during the Reformation* (Baltimore: Johns Hopkins University Press, 1995).

13. **Anna Janz:** Primarily based on the account of Anna Janz's death in *Martyrs Mirror.* Gerald Mast provided additional details from the German edition of *Martyrs Mirror* and from *Profiles of Anabaptist*

Women, edited by C. Arnold Snyder and Linda A. Huebert Hecht (Waterloo, ON: Wilfrid Laurier University Press, 1996).

14. **Dirk Willems:** Based entirely on the account in *Martyrs Mirror.*

15. **Veronika Löhans:** Adapted from "Behold the Lamb: A Brief History of the Moravian Church," by Peter Hoover (unpublished manuscript). For more on the Moravian mission in St. Thomas and particularly the life of Rebecca Freundlich, see Jon Sensbach's biography, *Rebecca's Revival: Creating Black Christianity in the Atlantic World* (Cambridge, MA: Harvard University Press, 2006).

16. **Jacob Hochstetler:** Based on William F. Hochstetler's introductory essay in *The Descendants of Jacob Hochstetler,* by Harvey Hostetler (Elgin, IL: Brethren Publishing House, 1912).

17. **Gnadenhütten:** Written by Craig Atwood, professor of history at Moravian College, for this book. Sources include *Moravian Women's Memoirs: Their Related Lives, 1750–1820,* edited by Katherine Faull (Syracuse, NY: Syracuse University Press, 1997); *A History of Bethlehem, Pennsylvania 1741–1892,* by Joseph Mortimer Levering (Bethlehem, PA: Times Publishing Company, 1903); and *The American Family of Rev. Obadiah Holmes,* by J. T. Holmes (Columbus, OH: 1915).

18. **Joseph and Michael Hofer:** Adapted from "The Martyrs of Alcatraz," by Duane Stoltzfus, *Plough Quarterly* 1 (Summer 2014). For a book-length account see Stoltzfus's *Pacifists in Chains* (Baltimore: Johns Hopkins University Press, 2013).

19. **Emanuel Swartzendruber:** Quotes and letter extracts are from *Writing Peace: The Unheard Voices of Great War Mennonite Objectors,* by Melanie Springer Mock (Telford, PA: Pandora Press, 2003).

20. **Regina Rosenberg:** Based on *Mennonitische Märtyrer der jüngsten Vergangenheit und der Gegenwart,* by Aron Toews (North Clearbrook, BC: 1949) and *Bilder aus Sowjetruszland,* by A. Kroeker (Hillsboro, KS: 1922).

21. **Eberhard and Emmy Arnold:** Sources include Emmy Arnold's memoir, *A Joyful Pilgrimage: My Life in Community* (Farmington,

PA: Plough, 1999) and Markus Baum's biography *Against the Wind: Eberhard Arnold and the Bruderhof* (Farmington, PA: Plough, 1998).

22. **Johann Kornelius Martens:** Based on a biographical essay by Peter Letkemann, translated by John Roth. Additional details came from Aron Toews's account in *Mennonite Martyrs* (Hillsboro, KS: Kindred Press, 1990).

23. **Ahn Ei Sook:** Based on Ahn Ei Sook's personal account of her resistance to the Japanese regime: *If I Perish* (Chicago: Moody Press, 1977).

24. **Jakob Rempel:** Based on several accounts of Rempel's life, primarily in *Mennonite Martyrs,* which includes primary sources and recollections from family members. Additional details came from Harold S. Bender's article on Rempel for *The Mennonite Encyclopedia.*

25. **Clarence Jordan:** Primarily based on Joyce Hollyday's biographical essay in *Clarence Jordan: Essential Writings* (Maryknoll, NY: Orbis Books, 2003). Additional details came from news articles published during Jordan's life and at the time of his death.

26. **Richard and Sabina Wurmbrand:** Drawn from three of Richard Wurmbrand's books: *In God's Underground* (Bartlesville, OK: Living Sacrifice Books, 1968), *Tortured for Christ* (Bartlesville, OK: Living Sacrifice Books, 1967) and *If Prison Walls Could Speak* (Bartlesville, OK: Living Sacrifice Books, 1972).

27. **Tulio Pedraza:** Based on Elizabeth Miller's article for the Bearing Witness Stories Project website (martyrstories.org). Miller interviewed Pedraza's family in May 2011 and also drew on "Hechos y crónicas de los menonitas en Colombia," Vol. 1, an unpublished manuscript by Raúl Pedraza Álvarez, and an unpublished 1952 essay by Gerald Stucky.

28. **Stanimir Katanic:** Based on an article by Marcia Lewandowski first published on the Bearing Witness Stories Project website. Lewandowski interviewed Katanic in Ohio in October 2014.

29. **Samuel Kakesa:** Based on a chapter on Kakesa's work in *The Jesus Tribe: Grace Stories from Congo's Mennonites,* by Vincent Ndandula

and Jim Bertsche (Elkhart, IN: Institute for Mennonite Studies, 2012). Additional details from *Light the World,* by Faith Eidse (Victoria, BC: Freisen Press, 2012).

30. **Kasai Kapata:** Based on *Profiles of Mennonite Faith* 23 (Spring 2003), which was adapted from "Kasai and Balakashi Kapata," by Byron Burkholder, in *They Saw His Glory: Stories of Conversion and Service* (Mennonite Brethren Board of Missions and Services, 1984).

31. **Meserete Kristos Church:** Based on Nathan Hege's book *Beyond Our Prayers* (Scottdale, PA: Herald Press, 1998).

32. **Sarah Corson:** Based on "Welcoming the Enemy," by Sarah Corson, *Sojourners* 12, no. 4 (April 1983).

33. **Alexander Men:** Adapted from Larry Woiwode's biographical essay "A Martyr Who Lives," in *Martyrs,* edited by Susan Bergman (Maryknoll, NY: Orbis Books, 1996). Additional details came from news articles published at the time of the investigation into Men's death.

34. **José Chuquín and Norman Tattersall:** Drawn from news coverage of Chuquín's and Tattersall's deaths. Additional information came from *Best Things in the Worst Times,* by Graeme Irvine (World Vision International, 1996).

35. **Katherine Wu:** Based on Sheldon Sawatsky's article on Wu's work, first published on the Bearing Witness Stories Project website. Additional information from "Beating of Taiwanese Mennonite Pastor Most Likely Due to Her Efforts to Provide Refuge to Child Prostitutes," by Carla Reimer and Chris Leuz, *The Mennonite* (1993).

36. **Ekklesiyar Yan'uwa a Nigeria:** Adapted from "Learning to Love Boko Haram," by Peggy Gish, *Plough Quarterly* 6 (Autumn 2015).

Acknowledgements

DOZENS OF PEOPLE contributed stories to this book, and many more gave advice. A few deserve special mention. John D. Roth and Elizabeth Miller of the Bearing Witness Stories Project conducted research, furnished and translated primary source materials, participated in the selection of stories, and provided editorial advice at every stage of the project. Paul J. Pastor and Kyle Rohane carefully edited (and often redrafted) each story to unify the tone and voice of the book as a whole.

The steering committee of the Bearing Witness Stories Project acted as a sounding board for many questions and suggestions. Several committee members even submitted stories that we've included here. We are especially thankful to Chester Weaver, Gerald Mast, Nelson Kraybill, Devin Manzullo-Thomas, and Johannes Dyck for their active role and to Lisa Weaver, Stephen Russell, and Peter Letkemann for their support.

We thank Duane Stoltzfus of Goshen College for permission to use his article on the Hutterite martyrs of World War I; Craig Atwood of Moravian College for researching and writing the Gnadenhütten story; Peter Hoover for permission to use his accounts of Veronika Löhans and Regina Rosenberg; Michael W. Holmes of Bethel University for his advice on the story of Polycarp; and Peggy Gish for her on-the-ground reporting on the persecuted church in Nigeria.

The Bearing Witness Stories Project

The Bearing Witness Stories Project invites Anabaptist communities worldwide to share their stories of costly discipleship, in hopes of inspiring greater faithfulness to Jesus Christ and strengthen the church's unity.

During the sixteenth century, more than three thousand Anabaptists died for their faith, and thousands more suffered torture, imprisonment, and banishment from their homes. Many of these stories were included in Thieleman van Braght's *Martyrs Mirror,* published in 1660. Although Anabaptists have continued to suffer for their faith since then, no comparable collection of stories has yet been made.

The aim of this project is to gather new stories from as many groups and individuals as want to participate, and to share them as widely as possible. The website martyrstories.org and this book are two steps towards making the stories accessible to people around the globe. The project focuses primarily on stories of Anabaptists who have willingly suffered, died, or experienced some significant deprivation for the cause of Christ, in the manner of the defenseless Christ, and who have expressed their faith through believer's baptism from within an identifiable ecclesial context, in a way that inspires faithfulness. If you have a story to contribute, please visit martyrstories.org for more details.

Other Titles from Plough

The Chronicle of the Hutterian Brethren, Volume 1
Begun over 430 years ago, the *Chronicle* is a fascinating account of early
Anabaptist martyrs and a record of Hutterite life from 1528 to 1665.

Discipleship: Living for Christ in the Daily Grind
J. Heinrich Arnold
Arnold guides readers toward leading Christ-like lives amid the stress
and strain of modern life.

The Early Christians: In Their Own Words
Eberhard Arnold
What did Christianity look like before it became an institution?

God's Revolution: Justice, Community, and the Coming Kingdom
Eberhard Arnold
Christ's truths can heal and save, but to do so, they must first turn our
lives upside down.

Homage to a Broken Man: The Life of J. Heinrich Arnold
Peter Mommsen
Can our wounds become our greatest gift? Discover a dramatic true
story of faith, forgiveness, sacrifice, and community.

Jesus and the Nonviolent Revolution
André Trocmé
Trocmé, known for saving thousands of Jews from the Nazis, explores
the implications of the social revolution that Jesus heralded.

Love Is Like Fire: The Confession of an Anabaptist Prisoner
Peter Riedemann
A twenty-three-year-old Christian wrote this spirited confession of
faith from a sixteenth-century Austrian dungeon.

My Search
Josef Ben-Eliezer
A young Jew escapes the Holocaust and Siberian exile, but that's only the beginning of a lifelong quest for peace.

Salt and Light: Living the Sermon on the Mount
Eberhard Arnold
Following the Sermon on the Mount is neither an ideal nor an ordeal, but an absolute necessity for followers of Jesus.

Seeking Peace: Notes and Conversations along the Way
Johann Christoph Arnold
Where can we find peace of heart and mind – with ourselves, with others, and with God? This book offers some surprising answers.

Why Forgive?
Johann Christoph Arnold
Arnold shares the stories of people who have earned the right to talk about forgiving, and about the peace they have found in doing so.

The Plough Publishing House
www.plough.com or e-mail: info@plough.com

151 Bowne Drive, PO BOX 398, Walden, NY 12586, USA
Brightling Rd, Robertsbridge, East Sussex, TN32 5DR UK
4188 Gwydir Highway, Elsmore NSW 2360 AUSTRALIA